What Children Need to Be

# Happy,
# Confident and
# Successful

*of related interest*

**Building Happiness, Resilience and Motivation in Adolescents**
**A Positive Psychology Curriculum for Well-Being**
*Tina Rae and Ruth MacConville*
ISBN 978 1 84905 261 0
eISBN 978 0 85700 548 9

**Working with Children and Teenagers Using Solution Focused Approaches**
**Enabling Children to Overcome Challenges and Achieve their Potential**
*Judith Milner and Jackie Bateman*
ISBN 978 1 84905 082 1
eISBN 978 0 85700 261 7

**Communication Skills for Working with Children and Young People**
**Introducing Social Pedagogy**
**3rd edition**
*Pat Petrie*
ISBN 978 1 84905 137 8
eISBN 978 0 85700 331 7

**A Short Introduction to Promoting Resilience in Children**
*Colby Pearce*
ISBN 978 1 84905 118 7
eISBN 978 0 85700 231 0
*JKP Short Introductions series*

**Helping Children to Build Self-Esteem**
**A Photocopiable Activities Book**
**2nd edition**
*Deborah M. Plummer*
*Illustrated by Alice Harper*
ISBN 978 1 84310 488 9
eISBN 978 1 84642 609 4

**The Big Book of Therapeutic Activity Ideas for Children and Teens**
**Inspiring Arts-Based Activities and Character Education Curricula**
*Lindsey Joiner*
ISBN 978 1 84905 865 0
eISBN 978 0 85700 447 5

**Cool Connections with Cognitive Behavioural Therapy**
**Encouraging Self-esteem, Resilience and Well-being in Children and Young People**
**Using CBT Approaches**
*Laurie Seiler*
ISBN 978 1 84310 618 0
eISBN 978 1 84642 765 7

Jeni Hooper

# What Children Need to Be
# Happy, Confident and Successful

## Step by Step Positive Psychology to Help Children Flourish

Jessica Kingsley *Publishers*
London and Philadelphia

First published in 2012
by Jessica Kingsley Publishers
116 Pentonville Road
London N1 9JB, UK
and
400 Market Street, Suite 400
Philadelphia, PA 19106, USA

*www.jkp.com*

**Library of Congress Cataloging in Publication Data**
Hooper, Jeni (Jenifer Susan), 1952-
  What children need to be happy, confident and successful : step by step
positive psychology to help children flourish / Jeni Hooper.
        p. cm.
  Includes bibliographical references and index.
  ISBN 978-1-84905-239-9 (alk. paper)
  1. Child psychology. 2. Positive psychology. 3. Child mental health. 4.
Child development. 5. Well-being. I. Title.
  BF721.H62 2012
  649'.6--dc23
                                2011042876

**British Library Cataloguing in Publication Data**
A CIP catalogue record for this book is available from the British Library

ISBN 978 1 84905 239 9
eISBN 978 0 85700 483 3

Printed and bound in Great Britain

# Contents

## Part I Positive Psychology and the Flourishing Programme

## Part II The Flourishing Programme

# LIST OF TABLES, FIGURES AND BOXES

## Tables

## Figures

## Boxes

# Preface

## HELPING CHILDREN TO FLOURISH

Do you want to ensure a child has a good life? Then you need to know about the factors which make a big impact on the quality of a child's life both now and in the future.

What makes children happy, confident and successful? Is it high intelligence? Is it having a stress-free and comfortable life? Perhaps it is the school you attend or the neighbourhood you live in? All these factors do count, of course, but they are not what makes the real and lasting difference. These factors are important but they are also hard to change.

The good news is that the real difference is in your hands. That difference is psychological wellbeing. Each and every adult can make a difference to a child and prepare them up for a life which is happy, confident and successful.

Psychological wellbeing is the umbrella term for a set of skills which every child needs to help them live their best life and to keep things on track when life gets tough. Questions about the quality of life have been debated since ancient times. In the past ten years a new branch of psychology has begun to put real evidence behind the philosophy and ideology that was all previous generations had to work with. Psychological wellbeing was previously the territory of self-help books, gurus and pundits. It was a fluffy, feel good subject which was hard to examine for evidence. Positive Psychology has done just that, taking ancient wisdom and examining its credentials and setting up research projects to explore the everyday beliefs we all hold dear. Some things have stood up to the test while others have crumbled.

This book brings together the key findings from Positive Psychology and combines them with essential knowledge from Child Psychology to give you a step by step guide to what every child needs to shape and manage their own lives and flourish.

# A QUICK GUIDE TO THE FLOURISHING PROGRAMME

This book introduces the Flourishing Programme, which is designed to help children achieve their personal potential in every area of their lives. Although most children are thriving on the opportunities which life puts their way many others need support. I developed the Flourishing Programme from cutting edge psychological research to take the trial and error out of helping children to find their best life.

## Who is it for?

A significant minority of children are not having the childhood they deserve. Increasing numbers of children have mental health issues, with anxiety and depression reaching almost epidemic proportions. Even children who appear to be progressing well can be unhappy with themselves and have low self-confidence.

The programme has been highly effective in improving wellbeing. You do not need to be a psychologist to use this programme and both professionals working with children and parents will find information and practical activities to guide them in nurturing wellbeing.

The target age group for the Flourishing Programme to be most effective is 3–11-year-olds, because early intervention is undoubtedly preferable to crisis intervention. However, you will find several case studies of adolescents who have benefited from the programme.

## Getting started

I recommend you read the book through once to get the complete picture before you start to put ideas into practice.

The First Steps to Flourishing Questionnaire provides an assessment of how well a child is progressing in the five key areas of wellbeing: personal strengths, emotional wellbeing, positive communication, learning strengths and resilience. Each key area is given a chapter, and these are topped and tailed by chapters which explore how to personalize the programme and how to promote independence as children mature.

Each chapter explores what we know about optimal wellbeing in a key area and then describes practical activities which help children to learn and practise skills which help them to be happier, more confident and more successful.

Each of the five sections of the questionnaire provides a baseline score between 0 and 40. The scores are not linked to age-related expectations because children differ widely in their wellbeing. The programme can be used independently where wellbeing is the major concern or alongside a personalized learning programme for a child with additional needs.

For all children the choice of activities from the appropriate section of the programme needs to take these three success factors into account:

- What is the smallest step which will make the biggest difference to give the child success?

- Is the activity of high interest and relevance to the child to engage them and create immediate impact on their life?

- Will this activity begin to resolve issues which negatively impact on the child's behaviour and relationships?

## Reviewing progress

The questionnaire can be updated at 6–12-week intervals to gauge progress. If you are using the programme by yourself do consider working with someone else to offer mutual support; there are ideas for co-coaching at the end of the book.

## Downloadable resources

All pages marked with a ✓ are available to download at www.jkp.com/catalogue/book/9781849052399/resources and www.jenihooper.com.

# Part I

# Positive Psychology and the Flourishing Programme

# What Do Children Need to Be Happy, Confident and Successful?

Positive Psychology is the science of wellbeing: a quest to find the universal truths which inform human progress and life satisfaction. It aims to discover and promote the factors which allow individuals and communities to thrive[1] and which play a vital role in getting young people off to a good start in life and prepares them for independence.

The World Health Organization (WHO) defines wellbeing[2] as 'a state in which the individual realizes his or her own abilities, can cope with the normal stresses of life, work productively and fruitfully and is able to make a contribution to the community' (p.19).

Every child has their own unique potential but not all children will blossom to develop their skills and build a life which is fulfilling and satisfying. For some children, the gulf between their potential and reality is enormous and the challenges in their lives can block the way to a good life. Yet, for many, small changes can make a big difference.

Later we will meet Toby, a boy who was really struggling but who recovered his enthusiasm and motivation through just such small changes to his everyday routine. For Toby and for all children the chance to reach for their potential is too important to be missed.

## BUILDING PSYCHOLOGICAL WELLBEING

This book is a guide to the essentials of wellbeing. It offers food for thought and practical ideas to everyone involved with children. Every adult who comes in contact with children can play their part in boosting a child's wellbeing. An understanding of the factors which promote psychological wellbeing is central both to preventing difficulties from arising and to providing an early intervention strategy for any child already in need of support.

## DECIDING WHAT IS IMPORTANT

As the body of scientific findings from psychology grows, it can be difficult to track down the key messages and to decide what will make a significant difference to wellbeing. As an applied psychologist, working directly in the community rather than in an academic setting, my work involves developing evidence-based practice. I have examined the research findings to distil them into key principles which were then translated into practical applications. In 2006 I started work on the Flourishing Programme, which is designed to promote psychological wellbeing in childhood. Over the past five years I have continued to review and refine the programme, working with parents and professionals to develop a practical guide to the psychological strengths children need for an enriching, meaningful and fulfilling life.

The chapters which follow introduce the Flourishing Programme, which shows you how to discover and build a child's unique personal talents. You will learn practical strategies for creating daily opportunities for children to practice and develop their strengths, specific ways to nurture positive emotions, and techniques for modelling how to manage negative thoughts and feelings.

## FACING THE FUTURE WITH CONFIDENCE

The wellbeing of children is a complex subject, depending as it does on the ability of both family and the community to meet children's needs. The western world has changed more radically in the past 50 years than in the previous 5000. These changes have brought huge advances in health care, technology and education, all of which have the potential to make life safer, more comfortable and to bring greater opportunities, but are not a guarantee of wellbeing. The pace of change also means that the world is more complicated and the choices young people need to make are more diverse than for previous generations.

The relationship between a better standard of living and improved life satisfaction is not a direct one. More people identified themselves as satisfied with their lives in a survey completed in 1940 than when the survey was repeated 50 years later.[3] Living in a country rich in resources and secure from war does not inevitably lead to psychological benefits.

The UNICEF survey of 2007,[4] *An Overview of Child Wellbeing in Rich Countries*, looked at six key indicators of child wellbeing including health, poverty, education and family life in the 21 richest countries. The results show that the United Kingdom was ranked lowest overall, with the United

States only one place above. Both countries were in the lowest 25 per cent across all six indicators. In both the United Kingdom and the United States marked inequalities exist between communities in terms of housing and employment which impacts on the wellbeing of adults disproportionately. For example, adult depression is higher in areas of poverty and unemployment. Addressing those social issues needs a political as well as a psychological solution. However, at an individual level Positive Psychology has much to offer parents and professionals to help them support children effectively.

## PLANNING FOR CHANGE

Although the need to support children's psychological wellbeing was widely accepted following the UNICEF survey, the specific strategies which would help parents and professionals work with children at an individual level to promote wellbeing were only outlined in a broad brush way in subsequent publications.[5] What is offered here is a more detailed guide to ways forward which can become a natural part of a child's daily life. The Flourishing Programme helps you actively build a child's capacity to flourish emotionally, socially and educationally.

Being a child isn't easy. There is so much you can't yet do and so much you aren't allowed to do. This can make the world seem a very complicated place. Indeed, the journey through childhood is complex. There are many skills to be learned, from walking and talking to learning how to make friends and how to study for exams successfully.

You may have read books on child development which tell you what to expect at different ages and stages in a child's life. This book takes a different perspective, exploring what it takes to help children remain happy, confident and be successful while negotiating each of the many milestones they will encounter on the route to adult independence. Making that progress depends upon psychological wellbeing to provide the inner strength and motivation to tackle each new stage in life with relish rather than frustration.

## BOOSTING PSYCHOLOGICAL WELLBEING

The chapters that follow will provide you with the knowledge and tools you need to nurture wellbeing. They will answer five key questions:

1. What is psychological wellbeing?
2. Why is it important?
3. Where does it come from?

4. What do people with psychological wellbeing do more of?

5. How can adults help a child to build their psychological wellbeing?

## THE BUILDING BLOCKS OF WELLBEING

The Flourishing Programme begins with a discussion of how to meet a child's individual needs, it then describes the five factors that make up the core areas of psychological wellbeing, and ends with a discussion of how to develop a child's independence. Part II of this book outlines the Flourishing Programme in detail and is divided as follows:

- Unique and personal: meeting a child's individual needs

- Factor 1: Personal strengths: the inner compass that guides our choices

- Factor 2: Emotional wellbeing: creating a positive balance

- Factor 3: Positive communication: building trust and fulfilling relationships

- Factor 4: Learning strengths: developing learning habits to motivate and get results

- Factor 5: Resilience: how to avoid roadblocks and bounce back from setbacks

- Developing independence: the journey through childhood

# Positive Psychology
## Understanding the
## Nature of Wellbeing

Part II will describe the Flourishing Programme in more detail. The Flourishing Programme weaves together key concepts from developmental psychology that help us to understand and support the major milestones of child development with Positive Psychology, which has explored the building blocks of wellbeing. To illustrate the programme in action we will meet Toby to find out what helped him turn things around.

Before we examine the Flourishing Programme in detail we will briefly explore the development of Positive Psychology and some of the earlier approaches to understanding wellbeing.

Both philosophy and psychology have applied themselves to explaining the nature of wellbeing – to identifying what creates a good and meaningful life. Philosophy has had a considerable head start on psychology. During the fourth century BC in Ancient Greece, Aristotle, a philosopher, contrasted the 'virtuous life' with the 'pleasant life'. The virtuous life or *eudaimonia* (derived from the concept *daimon*, or true nature) is where an individual's personal development is informed by higher goals which benefit not only themselves but others. Human flourishing was seen as striving towards your best self. Aristotle contrasts this with the pleasant life, or *hedonia*, which is focused solely on the individual's own physical and emotional needs at the present time.

While philosophy has considered what constitutes the 'good life' since ancient times, the scientific study of psychology was funded primarily to find ways to understand and alleviate complex needs such as mental illness and learning difficulties. Psychology in the twentieth century had become disconnected from most people's lives and offered little practical guidance for everyday living. While psychology was respected for championing the needs of the disadvantaged, its focus on supporting people with disabilities and mental health needs had distanced mainstream psychology from most people's lives.

Positive Psychology is a comparatively new branch of science launched in 1998 by Professor Martin Seligman as his presidential theme during his year of office as President of the American Psychological Society. Professor Seligman invited the psychological community to refocus scientific study onto what promotes optimal wellbeing. Martin Seligman was in a unique position to help psychology broaden its impact to the lives of the many rather than the few. His research career had been pivotal in identifying the mechanisms underlying depression.

Seligman and his colleagues identified the psychological process underlying depression which could be addressed directly. His team established that depression results from learned helplessness, a pessimistic mindset where people hold negative beliefs which deter them from attempting to improve their personal circumstances. As well as contributing to the development of Cognitive Behaviour Therapy, he had also had significant success with prevention programmes teaching the skills of optimism to challenge depressive thinking.[6] For Seligman, as for many others in the psychology community, it made sense to move from reacting to human misery to developing prevention and from professionalized and complex care to giving people the skills to manage their own lives effectively.

Seligman's was not the first examination of psychological wellbeing. From the 1950s Humanistic Psychology sought to identify what gave life depth and meaning. The approach of the Humanistic Psychologists was theoretical; describing and explaining what creates wellbeing. It had a huge impact on the development of counselling and therapy but less influence on the general population. Humanistic Psychology was particularly interested in examining motivation. Abraham Maslow developed perhaps the best known theory of motivation[7] from this period. His Hierarchy of Needs theory suggests that people have layers of needs which differ in their essential importance to survival. These are:

- physiological needs such as food and shelter
- safety and protection
- love and belonging: friendship and family
- esteem: confidence, achievement, respect
- self-actualization: individual creativity, problem solving, morality.

Maslow believed that the basic survival needs must be satisfied before other personal needs can be addressed. His theory suggests that when basic needs are unmet the individual becomes preoccupied with resolving or escaping that situation and cannot focus on the next level. Only when someone is safe, healthy and fully loved and accepted in their family and community can they move on to the personal growth and development stage, which he calls self-actualization – literally, finding yourself.

The appeal of Maslow's theory is its emphasis on the importance of the strong foundations provided by a mutually supportive society. His theory emerged into a post-war world which was busily rebuilding society and coping with the aftermath of the Great Depression. While no one would challenge his intentions, it is not clear that these levels of motivation are literally separate and hierarchical. We know that people can and do focus on self-actualizing goals, making substantial sacrifices of personal comfort and material wellbeing, while in pursuit of some powerfully important goal. However, on balance, his theory reminds us how debilitating prolonged deprivation or danger can be and how difficult it is to make progress in life if starving or under attack.

As young children develop, the desire to learn and achieve emerges in parallel with their emotional and physical needs. The need to explore and learn is a powerful drive which does not lie dormant until everything else in life is going well. As we will see in the chapter on personal strengths, a child's motivation to explore and learn needs to be given room to grow from the beginning, rather than being seen as the last thing on the priority list.

Positive Psychology differs from Humanistic Psychology in its scope and methodology. It has moved beyond theory building by using empirical research to inform our understanding of the factors which improve the quality of life. The last decade has seen a rich offering of insights into what people need to flourish. This has popularly been portrayed as happiness research but in fact goes far wider. Since its beginnings in 1998 Positive Psychology is now a rapidly developing field offering research evidence to answer key questions about wellbeing and life satisfaction which are relevant to us all. Positive Psychology has huge capacity to transform the lives of people who might otherwise not fulfil their potential.

Substantial research into subjective wellbeing has provided rich insights into the ingredients which improve the quality of people's lives. This has confirmed the Aristotelian view that the good life does not come from physical and emotional satisfaction alone. It seems that money really does not buy happiness and that hedonism, in the form of the modern pursuit of happiness through consumerism, is at best a short-term palliative for deeper needs which are not being addressed.

Research supports the view that the good or virtuous life requires finding a deeper meaning which satisfies our minds and the spiritual dimension of our lives as well as taking care of the physical and emotional. The spiritual dimension is no longer narrowly associated with religion, although those who practice a faith are more likely to report greater wellbeing.[8] Researchers have found that the spiritual dimension can be whatever gives someone meaning and purpose in their lives which rises above and beyond their own needs.

A seminal account of the essentials of psychological wellbeing can be found in Martin Seligman's latest book, *Flourish: A Visionary New Understanding of Happiness and Wellbeing and How to Achieve Them*.[9] Here Seligman identifies five core elements which constitute a flourishing life under the acronym of PERMA:

1. Positive Emotions

2. Engagement

3. Relationships

4. Meaning

5. Accomplishment

He identifies what flourishing adults are doing and what those with less than optimal lives can do to move things forward.

Children first need to learn these skills before they can flourish. Most research to date has focused on examining how mature and independent adults flourish and what they do to ensure their wellbeing. *What Children Need to Be Happy, Confident and Successful* goes one stage further to examine how these skills can be nurtured in childhood. The following chapters deepen our understanding of how quality adult support works in practice to create the ideal conditions for children to flourish. If this book has a motto it is this: 'You can make a difference – every adult matters in a child's life.'

# Wellbeing and the Flourishing Programme

Positive Psychology has now created a fundamental shift of emphasis from identifying and treating difficulties to identifying and building strengths. Over the past few years, the evidence of what works to help people reach their potential has been made widely available to adults, particularly via workplace training and coaching. However, applying this knowledge to children's development has been more limited.

If the concept of wellbeing is to be useful and practical it has to reach into every corner of our lives. It has to address not only the pinnacles of human achievement but also how to deal successfully with adversity. Psychological wellbeing is significantly more than happiness, despite the popular portrayal of Positive Psychology as pursuing happiness alone. It has at its core an understanding of how we learn and what drives growth. Personal development cannot be achieved without effort and some discomfort. Happiness and life satisfaction may be end results of wellbeing but it is the processes which drive wellbeing which we need to understand.

What can you do to create wellbeing? Would you call a life which has been made easy and where challenges have been avoided a good example of wellbeing? Or is wellbeing a more active and informed process of making choices which positively meet our own and others' essential needs?

Psychological wellbeing is not a state which ducks challenges. It includes the optimism that allows you to set your sights on a worthwhile goal and work towards it without any guarantee of success. Wellbeing also includes the power of hope that helps you travel through dark times and into a life better suited to your talents and temperament without giving up. Wellbeing also depends upon a capacity to appreciate the world around you, both natural and manmade so that you have the energy and commitment to maintain and improve your environment.

Psychological wellbeing is not just focused on the individual. The social side of wellbeing is equally important. The capacity for gratitude is a vital aspect of wellbeing that helps you focus on the positive emotions. Gratitude encourages you to nurture your relationships with the people in your life whose love, kindness and warmth has demonstrated their care for you and their willingness to help you reach for the stars.

# BUILDING STRENGTHS

Children flourish when they learn how to discover and build their strengths in each of the five key areas which are the focus of the Flourishing Programme.

## BOX 1   THE FIVE BUILDING BLOCKS OF PSYCHOLOGICAL WELLBEING

### 1. Personal strengths: the inner compass that guides our choices

Each child has skills and abilities which are highly motivating and which provide energy, enjoyment and ease of learning. *Personal strengths* identify what is important to us; they influence our personal values and beliefs which then inform the choices we make.

### 2. Emotional wellbeing: creating a positive balance

The positive emotions of happiness, optimism and gratitude have a major impact on *emotional wellbeing*. Our physical health, energy and emotional equilibrium are all positively accelerated by wellbeing and negatively affected by stress.

### 3. Positive communication: building trust and fulfilling relationships

Communication is more than words: body language, facial expression and voice tone all contribute to the message. *Positive communication* connects us to others and gives us the tools to understand and manage our own thoughts and feelings.

### 4. Learning strengths: developing habits to motivate and get results

The future requires creative, adaptable life-long learners who can recognize and work to their strengths. New research has proved the dynamic impact of a growth mindset: a set of learning strategies which significantly improve learning and problem solving.

### 5. Resilience: how to avoid roadblocks and bounce back from setbacks

The ability to hold fast emotionally under pressure and to think clearly to search for solutions is the essence of resilience. *Resilience* allows us to redress the impact of external stress and cope with personal mistakes and disappointments. It includes forward thinking to avoiding situations which may be harmful and acting promptly to manage the unforeseen.

Every child is different and the basis of the Flourishing Programme is to adapt the information and ideas to match each child's individual needs. Similarly your own personal values and life experience are a rich resource to help you guide and mentor children. This book aims to support rather than to supplant your natural style.

Psychological wellbeing does not result from a fixed blueprint which follows a one size fits all formula; it is a set of principles, which like a set of ingredients can be adapted to create your own recipe. Just as every child is different, so is every adult, and the nurturing relationship which develops between you will be at its best when both adult and child feel able to be themselves.

## ENJOYING WELLBEING

Psychological wellbeing is a zest for life which stems from knowing who you are and what you are capable of achieving. Wellbeing is a positive sense of yourself that helps you make good choices. You know what suits you and also have the inner strength to bounce back from setbacks.

If people were cars, wellbeing would be like a finely tuned and well maintained engine which can coast along an open road but equally well shift gears to manage a steep and winding road in bad weather. Obviously, having psychological wellbeing doesn't guarantee that the world will always go your way but it does equip you to manage both the best and the worst of times. We cannot expect to be happy all the time but we can learn the skills to manage our wellbeing and lead satisfying lives whatever comes our way.

## THE CHILD SUPPLIES THE POWER BUT ADULTS DO THE STEERING

Children flourish when they find their strengths. Strengths are ways of thinking, feeling and behaving that create positive energy and drive our best performance. This will create a route to natural and easy development, which is comfortable for a child and leads to success.

Helping children to learn the skills which underlie positive wellbeing will ensure that they discover what brings out the best in themselves. For every child this will be different but the underlying process of gaining self-awareness and developing positive emotional, learning and social skills remains the same. As children mature they will be increasingly able to manage their own wellbeing by knowing what works for them. Gaining this self-knowledge depends on close relationships with adults who understand them intimately and can guide them to make authentic choices which promote happiness, confidence and success. The principles for helping each child to discover their strengths are explored in each chapter.

## THE IMPORTANCE OF CHILDHOOD WELLBEING

Learning about yourself and the skills you need for life is an important part of childhood. Growing in confidence and self-knowledge takes time and a strong network of support. The lives that children lead now are more stressful and demanding than in previous generations. Children are bombarded with expectations from many sources: home and school, their peer group and what they see in the media. These expectations are not always aligned with each other and conflicting expectations can lead to confusion. The uncertainty about direction and boundaries creates the potential for stress, anxiety and unhappiness.

Despite the pressures from the world around them, nature usually gets children off to a good start. Children are natural explorers. They start life with boundless energy and a powerful desire to test their own abilities. They want to know more about the world around them and they are very determined. Can I crawl to that shelf to get that brightly coloured toy? Can I climb that tree to see the world from a different angle? Can I build a go-cart that moves really fast? This book explores how to support and channel that exuberance so that children flourish and have bullet-proof psychological wellbeing.

## AVOIDING THE DOWNHILL SLIDE

For too many children, as they leave the toddler years their positive energy and curiosity seems to drain away. They become restless, unhappy or easily bored. Their natural zest for life is dimmed and their sense of purpose is lost. Sometimes this change results from adverse health or life experiences but more often the cause is more subtle and linked to the pressures of a busy world which can pull them in too many directions which are not in tune with their needs. This book explores how you can reignite a child's sparkle and enthusiasm for life through gentle, positive approaches to nurture psychological wellbeing.

## HELPING CHILDREN TO FLOURISH

In my work as a child psychologist and parent coach I meet children who have untapped potential and are not moving forward. They are not necessarily children with significant special needs or from families in crisis. They are restless and unhappy and underperforming in school but the reasons for this are not clear. Their family life is supportive and their schools are working hard to help them progress but somehow the fire within is not burning brightly. These children are healthy children with considerable untapped potential.

The principles in this book also apply to children with more complex needs but you may wish to work alongside others to plan a programme of support which will have an extensive reach through every aspect of the child's life. I use this programme in my own multi-agency work with children with complex needs.

## MOVING FORWARD

For children to be happy, and successful, their strengths need to be in daily use. Most children and a great many adults are not sufficiently aware of their own strengths, so they are playing and learning in an ad hoc way that is not right for them. As children begin to understand their strengths and make choices that suit them they spend their time more enjoyably and success comes easily and naturally to them. When adults are confident in discovering and building a child's strengths then progress has a natural momentum. For most children just making small changes will make a big difference, as you will see when we meet Toby.

# Toby's Story

When I first met Toby he was a very unhappy eight-year-old boy. He was doing virtually no work at school and was often bad tempered and uncommunicative at home. He had not always felt this way. Until recently he had seemed to enjoy school, especially when his class were given practical projects where he could investigate a topic or make things. Now he was a changed boy, he dawdled on the way to school and when he got home he was reluctant to talk about what he had done at school that day. His parents were deeply puzzled and worried. The family had hoped an outside interest might help him and had arranged music lessons for him. These got off to a good start but his enthusiasm soon tailed off. He started to learn the piano but hated it and then moved on to the guitar but this also seemed to be a disappointment. Both school and family described him as unmotivated but were unsure how to take this forward. His parents consulted me to ask 'What can we do to motivate him?'

## AN UNDERCURRENT OF ANXIETY

Toby was initially reluctant to talk to me when I met him but brightened up when I asked him what he enjoyed. He showed me a story he had written about monsters but said it was more difficult to do his best work in school as 'teachers tell you what to write about'. Further exploration revealed that his class were regularly tested to formally monitor progress. The school was conscientious about improving children's progress but for Toby this created an undercurrent of anxiety. He had worried about being tested and had gradually lost confidence in himself because his results seemed to disappoint everyone, although originally he had been trying hard. Now Toby wasn't sure what to do to please adults, which was why he was slow to start work and this avoidance strategy seemed to protect him from feeling a failure. 'If you don't try, you can't fail.' Now he was rarely able to feel proud of his achievements because the pace of lessons moved on before he felt confident of what he was doing.

## GETTING THINGS RIGHT NOW IS A PREPARATION FOR THE FUTURE

Toby, as a lively eight-year-old boy, found thinking about the future rather difficult. He knew it was important because adults seemed so concerned about what would be useful to him in later life. Toby was more interested in what would enrich his life today.

Toby's music lessons had started out as fun but both the piano and guitar lessons had quickly become a chore with lots of repetitive practice which didn't sound like real music to him. There was no joy in the moment. Because he was so busy all the time the chance to play freely was also in scare supply. He had little time to himself between school, homework and music practice. Toby understandably was bewildered and a bit fed up. He had given up trying because 'the more you do, the more they want' as he mournfully told me.

## THE SOLUTION

Toby was a boy with untapped potential who needed to connect with his strengths. A three-part strategy was agreed involving his writing, music and free time for creative play. The improvement in his attitude was swift. Things began to turn around when we identified how his interest in imaginative writing and music could be developed. Toby was invited to join a story writing group in school. The teacher encouraged the group to read their finished stories to a younger class. He learned useful skills about writing for an audience and the interest the younger children showed gave him encouragement. Out of school his family enrolled him in drum classes, which suited his energetic temperament better than the piano or guitar. Drumming also developed his sense of rhythm and attention skills. Time was protected every day for free play either with his friends or at home. Toby was not only having more fun but he was learning and was much more cheerful and relaxed.

## FOCUSING ON TOBY'S STRENGTHS

Toby's school and his family both acknowledged that he needed more time to enjoy being an eight-year-old. They accepted that a slower pace of learning would consolidate his achievements. Although everyone had started with good intentions of helping Toby achieve his potential, the external pressures had backfired, causing him to feel undervalued and anxious. By focusing on Toby's strengths and allowing him to savour these positive experiences new relationships emerged which were positive and supportive. Toby began to flourish; he was confident of his own strengths and now knew he could rely on adults to listen to his views so that his learning became a shared experience.

## WHAT HAD GONE WRONG?

So why did the world seem such a tough place through Toby's young eyes? He had a family who loved him and encouraged him with his hobbies. He attended a school which was focusing on getting the best results for their pupils. But, despite this, Toby felt anxious and confused, he believed he was disappointing everyone and saw their helpful advice as criticism. Toby felt under pressure and was more aware of his 'failures' than his strengths.

## SMALL STEPS, BIG CHANGES

Actually, Toby needed only small shifts in the messages he received from adults to make rapid progress. Once everyone was focusing on his strengths and using those abilities to help him succeed, his enthusiasm returned.

## DEVELOPING TOBY'S CORE STRENGTHS

For Toby we worked on three core strengths where previously the negative messages he was receiving were draining his enthusiasm.

### Emotional wellbeing

- Toby needed more free time to reset his emotional thermostat and hang out, just having fun.
- Ensuring he had at least an hour's free play a day outside of school gave him the chance to do things to please himself.

- Consequently he became much more positive and willing to engage in all the activities carefully chosen for him by his family and teachers.

## Positive communication

- Praise for his efforts was increased.
- Toby needed to hear more positive feedback which was clear and specific.

## Learning strengths

- Joining the story writing group made use of his imaginative strengths and created a practical outcome for his work.
- His interest in music was re-examined and drums provided a lively and exciting option.

# First Steps to Flourishing Questionnaire

This questionnaire is designed to gather information on a child's wellbeing. It assumes that flourishing results from what you do which reflects what you think and feel. By observing children's actions you can assess the extent and range of their flourishing behaviours. You can use it to help you identify areas of strengths and areas where support would be valuable. This questionnaire is suitable for children aged three and above, although the younger the child is the earlier they will be on their developmental path to flourishing. Younger children are just starting out and this will give you pointers for support.

Scoring

| Never | Rarely | Sometimes | Frequently | Always |
|-------|--------|-----------|------------|--------|
| 0 | 1 | 2 | 3 | 4 |

✓

# Personal strengths

| | 0 | 1 | 2 | 3 | 4 |
|---|---|---|---|---|---|
| 1. Keeps busy in play/activities for extended period of time | | | | | |
| 2. Gets very absorbed in any chosen activity | | | | | |
| 3. Prefers to make own choices for play | | | | | |
| 4. Shows increased energy and enthusiasm when engaged in own play | | | | | |
| 5. Rarely claims to be bored/unsure what to do | | | | | |
| 6. Seeks adult support for practical information or equipment but otherwise independent | | | | | |
| 7. Is open to new experiences and activities and likes to find new ways of doing things | | | | | |
| 8. Is self-motivated when tasks are relevant and purposeful | | | | | |
| 9. Sets own goals to measure progress on special projects | | | | | |
| 10. Eager to tell others about areas of special interest | | | | | |

Totals

| 0 | 1 | 2 | 3 | 4 |
|---|---|---|---|---|

Comments . . . . . . . . . . . . . . . . . . . . . . . . . . . . . . . . . . . . . . . . . . . . . . . . . . . . . . . . .
. . . . . . . . . . . . . . . . . . . . . . . . . . . . . . . . . . . . . . . . . . . . . . . . . . . . . . . . . . . . . .
. . . . . . . . . . . . . . . . . . . . . . . . . . . . . . . . . . . . . . . . . . . . . . . . . . . . . . . . . . . . . .
. . . . . . . . . . . . . . . . . . . . . . . . . . . . . . . . . . . . . . . . . . . . . . . . . . . . . . . . . . . . . .
. . . . . . . . . . . . . . . . . . . . . . . . . . . . . . . . . . . . . . . . . . . . . . . . . . . . . . . . . . . . . .

✓

# Emotional wellbeing

| | | 0 | 1 | 2 | 3 | 4 |
|---|---|---|---|---|---|---|
| 1. | Seeks adult support and comfort when extremely upset | | | | | |
| 2. | Can settle with adult support within 5 to 10 minutes | | | | | |
| 3. | Will use own strategies to self-calm when mildly upset | | | | | |
| 4. | Can go for a week or more without tantrums or outbursts | | | | | |
| 5. | Has days when moods are more positive than negative | | | | | |
| 6. | Responds well to the positive emotional ethos created by others | | | | | |
| 7. | Moods can be lifted by shared activity | | | | | |
| 8. | Shows confidence in new situations and is rarely anxious | | | | | |
| 9. | Is lively and shows interest in the world | | | | | |
| 10. | Can move away from stressful situations to avoid being drawn into trouble | | | | | |

Totals

| 0 | 1 | 2 | 3 | 4 |
|---|---|---|---|---|
| | | | | |

Comments . . . . . . . . . . . . . . . . . . . . . . . . . . . . . . . . . . . . . . . . . . . . . . . . . . . . . . . . . .
. . . . . . . . . . . . . . . . . . . . . . . . . . . . . . . . . . . . . . . . . . . . . . . . . . . . . . . . . . . . . . . . .
. . . . . . . . . . . . . . . . . . . . . . . . . . . . . . . . . . . . . . . . . . . . . . . . . . . . . . . . . . . . . . . . .
. . . . . . . . . . . . . . . . . . . . . . . . . . . . . . . . . . . . . . . . . . . . . . . . . . . . . . . . . . . . . . . . .
. . . . . . . . . . . . . . . . . . . . . . . . . . . . . . . . . . . . . . . . . . . . . . . . . . . . . . . . . . . . . . . . .

✓

# Positive communication

| | 0 | 1 | 2 | 3 | 4 |
|---|---|---|---|---|---|
| 1. Shares news, ideas and personal views | | | | | |
| 2. Listens attentively when in conversation | | | | | |
| 3. Tunes into and follows suggestions and instructions from an adult in charge | | | | | |
| 4. Can share own viewpoint and negotiate with someone without aggression | | | | | |
| 5. Non-verbal communication matches words avoiding mixed messages | | | | | |
| 6. Responds to others in a friendly, encouraging way | | | | | |
| 7. Seeks out others for play and companionship | | | | | |
| 8. Shows humour in play and conversation | | | | | |
| 9. Is aware of and sensitive to others' feelings | | | | | |
| 10. Will help someone without being asked | | | | | |

Totals

| 0 | 1 | 2 | 3 | 4 |
|---|---|---|---|---|
| | | | | |

Comments . . . . . . . . . . . . . . . . . . . . . . . . . . . . . . . . . . . . . . . . . . . . . . . . . . .
. . . . . . . . . . . . . . . . . . . . . . . . . . . . . . . . . . . . . . . . . . . . . . . . . . . . . . . . .
. . . . . . . . . . . . . . . . . . . . . . . . . . . . . . . . . . . . . . . . . . . . . . . . . . . . . . . . .
. . . . . . . . . . . . . . . . . . . . . . . . . . . . . . . . . . . . . . . . . . . . . . . . . . . . . . . . .
. . . . . . . . . . . . . . . . . . . . . . . . . . . . . . . . . . . . . . . . . . . . . . . . . . . . . . . . .

✓

# Learning strengths

|  | 0 | 1 | 2 | 3 | 4 |
|---|---|---|---|---|---|
| 1. Is curious and interested in new activities |  |  |  |  |  |
| 2. Likes to talk about own interests with others |  |  |  |  |  |
| 3. Becomes fully absorbed when a topic is of personal interest |  |  |  |  |  |
| 4. Is confident when trying something new |  |  |  |  |  |
| 5. Seeks adult support to help problem solve but otherwise independent |  |  |  |  |  |
| 6. Prefers to judge progress by personal goals |  |  |  |  |  |
| 7. Rarely judges progress in comparison with others |  |  |  |  |  |
| 8. Seldom gives up when something is difficult |  |  |  |  |  |
| 9. Able to make a sustained effort when task challenging but achievable |  |  |  |  |  |
| 10. Works to satisfy self with praise or good marks of secondary importance |  |  |  |  |  |

Totals

| 0 | 1 | 2 | 3 | 4 |
|---|---|---|---|---|

Comments ...........................................................................
..........................................................................................
..........................................................................................
..........................................................................................
..........................................................................................

✓

# Resilience

| | 0 | 1 | 2 | 3 | 4 |
|---|---|---|---|---|---|
| 1. Is optimistic about the future | | | | | |
| 2. Has plans and believes in making things happen | | | | | |
| 3. Can positively reframe a difficult situation to see 'the bright side' | | | | | |
| 4. Shows effort and persistence in working towards personal goals | | | | | |
| 5. Can put aside short-term distractions to follow longer-term goals | | | | | |
| 6. Will ask for support when under pressure but retains responsibility for resolving problems | | | | | |
| 7. Makes compromises and adapts to others' wishes to maintain harmony | | | | | |
| 8. Shows acts of kindness/generosity to others | | | | | |
| 9. Shows forgiveness and willingness to resolve disputes | | | | | |
| 10. Shows gratitude for support and kindness from others | | | | | |

Totals

| 0 | 1 | 2 | 3 | 4 |
|---|---|---|---|---|
| | | | | |

Comments . . . . . . . . . . . . . . . . . . . . . . . . . . . . . . . . . . . . . . . . . . . . . . . . . . . . . . . . . . . . . .
. . . . . . . . . . . . . . . . . . . . . . . . . . . . . . . . . . . . . . . . . . . . . . . . . . . . . . . . . . . . . . . . . . . . . . .
. . . . . . . . . . . . . . . . . . . . . . . . . . . . . . . . . . . . . . . . . . . . . . . . . . . . . . . . . . . . . . . . . . . . . . .
. . . . . . . . . . . . . . . . . . . . . . . . . . . . . . . . . . . . . . . . . . . . . . . . . . . . . . . . . . . . . . . . . . . . . . .
. . . . . . . . . . . . . . . . . . . . . . . . . . . . . . . . . . . . . . . . . . . . . . . . . . . . . . . . . . . . . . . . . . . . . . .

✓

## Interpreting scores

Score each section to identify comparative areas of strengths. The highest score in any section is 40 and the lowest score is 0. Where a child receives a low score on any question this is an appropriate an area for support. It is not unusual for children to have an uneven pattern of scores reflecting greater strengths in some areas than in others. However, where a child has low scores across all five areas of wellbeing you will need to decide where support would have the greatest impact. In my experience focusing first on building personal strengths gives children a sense of mastery and competence which raises confidence and builds trust with the supporting adult. It creates a win–win situation for both of you.

Each chapter in Part II identifies the particular strength builders which contribute to wellbeing. There are no established norms for age groups and it is likely that younger children will be at an earlier stage of developing their strengths and achieve overall lower scores.

Observational comments can be particularly helpful in capturing the personal detail of how a child responds.

✓

# Part II

# The Flourishing Programme

# Unique and Personal
## Meeting a Child's Individual Needs

### FINDING THE POTENTIAL IN EVERY CHILD

It is being self-aware that sets human beings apart from other creatures. Conscious awareness gave our ancestors a huge evolutionary advantage based on the capacity to think, plan and create new opportunities. The power of thought makes it possible to manage our environment and keep ourselves safe from harm. We don't have massive strength, flesh-tearing teeth or razor sharp claws, just a powerful brain. The capacity to think creates a fierce independence of mind which has long-term advantages for adult independence and wellbeing. However, in the short term that feisty spirit in the child does not make life easy for adults.

Children have minds of their own and nature gives them great reserves of energy to propel them to explore and learn. You may have read books on managing children's behaviour which sound more like a manual for taming wild animals. The techniques used are often based on the principles of reward and punishment which can be highly effective in training your dog. Your dog instinctively wants to please you anyway as you are 'top dog', that's how pack animals understand the world. It works brilliantly for dogs. We human beings are deeply sociable but we are not pack animals and independence of mind is one of our strongest assets. We need therefore to understand and nurture each child's strengths rather than try to tame them and break their spirit.

When I first trained as a psychologist Behaviourism was a powerful influence in universities. Behaviourist theory suggested that all behaviour was shaped by the simple process of rewards and punishment. The assumption was that any behaviour that was rewarded would increase and if it was punished it would decrease. The inner child was never considered. Our understanding of human behaviour is now much more rich and complex. We know that when people are able to make choices that are personally fulfilling, this leads to a greater sense of personal wellbeing than when they only work for external rewards.[10]

Bringing up children calls upon leadership skills and strategies; the command and control approach, where you are the omnipotent leader using fear and favour to enforce your authority works very poorly with children. Nor is the reverse any better, where you allow the child to lead you. Inevitably a child doesn't know much yet about what is good for them and everyone gets extremely frustrated.

The Flourishing Programme identifies what children need for healthy, happy development which will help you discover and nurture any child's unique potential. Caring for and guiding young humans is very demanding. The human brain takes a long time to mature and children need support and guidance which adapts to their own increasing competence and independence. The path to adult life is a long haul but offers an incredibly exciting journey.

There is no comparison with this extended childhood in the animal world. This is because both animals and birds are born with built-in instincts and skills which mature quickly and easily with far less adult support. Human development is richer and more complex and therefore slower. In order to have the highly adaptable brain required for learning the local language, the skills and the culture, children are born with few instincts and no pre-set patterns of behaviour. They have to learn everything they need and this happens slowly over the whole of childhood. To achieve this growth children need to retain the drive to explore and have the strong will required for such an active learning journey. We should celebrate this independence of mind and nurture it so that each child can use their potential productively.

## THE JOYS AND THE CHALLENGES

Every child needs to learn about the world and know how to make decisions which are positive and which keep them safe. They learn this directly from what adults teach them and indirectly through what they observe. There will be times when the partnership between adult and child is a delight but at other times the power struggle can be undeniably exhausting. The child's energy may be prodigious but their spirit is small and fragile and requires sensitive support and nurturing to grow into a strong and resilient adult. It is the quality of relationships with adults which is the key to progress and to nurturing psychological wellbeing. The Flourishing Programme is both a guide to what children need for their wellbeing and a practical manual for adults.

## BOX 2 THE SIX CORE PRINCIPLES FOR NURTURING INDIVIDUAL WELLBEING

### 1. Every child is different

Each child has a unique combination of talents, temperament and vitality which shapes how they respond to the world as they find it. In young children their temperament is what we notice first: are they bold or shy, lively or quiet, confident or rather anxious? This will shape how the child interacts both with the environment and with people. Knowing the child is the first principle on which this programme depends. Helping each child to discover and express their potential depends upon working with what is there, rather than what you expect to find.

### 2. Children are not like clay waiting to be moulded

Human beings start life knowing nothing, and have huge potential to develop into unique individuals, but they are not clay ready to be moulded. Our current understanding of individual differences suggests that these result from the interaction of genes and environment in equal measure. Any attempt to mould a child to someone's personal blueprint is likely to lead to disappointment and frustration on both sides. Talents which are developed early through parental pressure do not always sustain their promise, particularly if the adult's motivation is greater than the child's. Not only does the talent not maintain its initial promise but the child's wellbeing can be seriously affected.[11] Children driven under pressure react with the stress response, wanting either to escape or else opting out and refusing to do anything. Even when their talent does survive, the relationship with the demanding adult may not. Vanessa Mae, the violinist, described how she sacked her manager mother: 'How I broke free of the gilded cage my mother kept me in.'[12]

### 3. Unique potential can be discovered and nurtured

Getting to know a child, like building any relationship, needs time together to tune into the child's interests and share experiences. Finding the time to do this can be difficult. Some commentators have suggested that families consider a change of gear to slow life down and focus on priorities[13] while others advocate making regular time available for each child with each parent.[14] In schools teaching methods acknowledge the importance of personalized learning and engaging the child as an active and enthusiastic learner.

When I was teaching six-year-olds, not long after I had graduated, I was touched and surprised as a naive 22-year-old by how hard each child worked to get my undivided attention. It was not easy to keep all the plates spinning but each child positively sparkled when I managed to really listen to them or show that I had noticed some special achievement.

Finding ways to give a child your undivided attention whether as a parent or a professional is vital to both understanding them and to building a relationship of influence. Children primarily want to be known and understood as unique individuals.

### 4. Adults act as a mirror to reflect back the child's best self

Children learn to understand themselves from the reactions of others around them. The developing child needs a mirror to reflect back their actions and their achievements so they can see themselves more clearly. You are that mirror and for most of the first decade of childhood children know what they want but not how well things are progressing. Even when children begin to develop their own powers of reflection to consider their progress, the appreciation and positive feedback adults offer keeps them positive and confident.

### 5. Mentoring and role models

Mentoring is a supportive relationship where someone with greater experience encourages someone to develop their full potential. The mentor is able to focus on the needs of the other to help them find out how to make progress. A mentor is appreciative of the potential of the individual they are supporting. A mentor encourages self-help and initiative. Mentoring is less about applying universal skills of parenting or teaching and more about education in its original sense which is about 'drawing out' the potential each person has inside them.

### 6. Understanding and meeting your own needs

A good relationship with a child is radically different from a balanced relationship between two adults where each can mutually support the other's needs. A child may like you, if you know them professionally, or love you as a family member but their emotional connection to you doesn't always lead to the give and take that we expect in healthy adult relationships. Once we acknowledge that a different set of rules apply we are more likely to ensure that our own needs get met elsewhere while we teach children to become socially sensitive and capable of understanding others' needs. Many children find themselves faced with unrealistic expectations from their parents now that families are smaller and parents have fewer close relationships to support their own emotional needs. We explore how you can identify your own relationship strengths when we look at positive communication.

Now that we have considered the uniqueness of every child we will explore what skills a child needs to discover their potential and make a fulfilling life.

Factor 1

# Personal Strengths
## The Inner Compass that Guides Our Choices

### Overview

Personal strengths are central to psychological wellbeing; they express who we are and what is important to us and inform the choices we make. Helping children to discover and use their unique personal strengths enables them to find their personal identity and express their individuality.

- Personal strengths are those interests and abilities which have strong appeal to the child.

- Personal strengths are motivating because they bring both success and satisfaction.

- Developing and using personal strengths creates positive energy and a desire to continue to engage with building this skill or knowledge.

- Personal strengths enable children to discover the world and to learn about themselves more effectively.

- Personal strengths provide positive experiences ('I did that,' 'I made that happen'), which create a sense of autonomy and competence.

- Personal strengths when practised daily become a personal toolbox to promote achievement.

# UNDERSTANDING PERSONAL STRENGTHS

## How personal strengths drive motivation

Human survival has always depended on a desire to make things happen. A powerful urge to survive drives us forward to meet our needs for food, safety and good company. It fights against us sitting doing nothing and makes us restless and looking for action unless we are either extremely tired or able to 'rest on our laurels' because we have just done something to be proud of.

Every child starts life with a burning desire to explore and learn; an inner spark of curiosity that needs to be satisfied. Supporting and channelling this desire to be busy and involved creates the difference between success and aimless experimentation. Children want to be capable and successful but without sensitive and informed adult support their efforts can be haphazard and frustrating. Education is one way to channel this desire for knowledge and achievement but children need outlets for their personal strengths in every aspect of their lives.

## What do we mean by strength?

Strength is a word which is associated with physical action and competence. If we look to a dictionary definition we find a broader definition:

*A strength is something which is regarded as beneficial or a source of power.*

Strengths are important because they enable children to discover and use their personal power positively and productively. Strengths are dynamic and will grow with regular use. When something is a strength, we long to use it. When we are actively using that strength it energizes us and absorbs our attention. We go for it 100 per cent: our effort, our attention, our thinking, and our physical energy are all fully engaged. If we meet a challenge we want to find a solution. How can we help children to experience that motivation and satisfaction in their daily lives?

Personal strengths are profoundly important because they become part of our personal identity. Children who do not discover their strengths can become anxious and uncertain or frustrated and aimless. The dynamic energy that we all have within us needs to be channelled and nurtured so that each child finds what works for them. This is what is meant by the concept of strengths.

Strengths are more than natural ability, which might lie dormant below the surface, as a potential, without ever being used. Strengths are something that we choose to use and we gain energy and satisfaction from doing so.

Each strength comes from a fourfold combination of ability, motivation, effort and social support.

## Strength = ability + motivation + effort + social support

We met Toby earlier; his story illustrates that abilities don't automatically become strengths. They need an outlet and they need support. A child's development is dependent on social stimulation and practical experience. For a personal strength to be realized the environment needs to be right. Toby had become confused by the mixed messages from adults and had begun to doubt himself. Some gentle, light touch support and room to explore and 'go it alone' reignited Toby's enthusiasm. His strengths began to grow again and gave him immense satisfaction.

## Understanding motivation: Self Determination Theory

Self Determination Theory (SDT) developed by Deci and Ryan offers an inspiring view of the central role of individual motivation by recognizing the importance of mastery and achievement. Their research started in the mid 1970s and has gained acceptance within the scientific community through over 30 years of research. Dan Pink's book, *Drive*, explores how Deci and Ryan's theory could have a revolutionary impact on motivation, particularly in the workplace.[15] Self Determination Theory deserves to be more widely known. Although it preceded the launch of Positive Psychology it sits well alongside more recent developments. SDT examines what people need to initiate and sustain the process of personal growth.

Deci and Ryan's research suggests that there are three important biological needs which create the drive towards growth. These three factors influence all our choices and determine our behaviour. When these needs are blocked or limited there is a powerful negative impact on personal growth.

Self Determination Theory stresses the importance of personal motivation to our wellbeing. When people are able to choose and control more aspects of their lives they tend to show more enthusiasm, stay involved for longer and achieve a better outcome. Children need the opportunity to find out about themselves and test their limits as well as a chance to explore and learn about the world.

## BOX 3 THE THREE FACTORS THAT CREATE WELLBEING

### 1. Competence

The need to be effective and capable of contributing to the world we are in. If someone feels incompetent or helpless but unable to deal with this, their motivation is seriously affected. Children are especially vulnerable to feelings of incompetence because they have so much to learn.

### 2. Autonomy

The urge to manage our own lives and act in harmony with our selves. This is a desire for personal coherence and authenticity rather than a desire for separateness and independence from others. The modern world allows less freedom and autonomy to children than previous generations in order to protect them and guide them.

### 3. Relatedness

The need to give and receive contact and loving care. This need to belong gives individuals security and recognition.

## *The child provides the drive while the adults do the steering*

We see this happening when young children take their first steps, eager to do it for themselves. Similarly the drive is visible in the feisty determination of the two-year-old who knows what they want and will not give in easily when told no. The energy and determination that young children have is an essential driver of human potential.

Positive Psychology has explored how this drive emerges and unfolds into personal strengths. Each of us has unique dynamic strengths which shape both our character and our learning style. These strengths influence our values and beliefs, our thinking and learning, and how we relate to others in our social world.

Our strengths decide the choices we make about how we like to spend our time. Strengths form the foundation of our personal identity and reflect the competence and autonomy strands of Self Determination Theory.

Every child needs to find their dynamic power and be supported to build their strengths so they can be competent and successful. The need for autonomy and competence is central to our wellbeing and without it we feel thwarted and dissatisfied.

## Avoiding 'learned helplessness'

Children who don't excel in any particular area compared with their peers may struggle to gain recognition. They have a particularly urgent need for more opportunities to use their preferred strengths to build their wellbeing from within. All children need to know they can make things happen in their world. As adults we can make sure that children avoid 'learned helplessness', which happens when someone feels unable to make a positive impact in their world.

As an educational psychologist I have worked with both special schools and mainstream schools, helping them support young people with severe and complex needs. Every teacher and parent knows the vital importance of giving children with additional needs a life which is rich in experience and which helps them to feel capable and valued. These young people do have preferred strengths, they have things that they love to do and which give them satisfaction. While it is important to help children learn new skills which they find difficult, they will only flourish when they have the chance to do things which give them personal satisfaction. We have to get the balance right.

Hayley has severe learning difficulties which have affected her development significantly. She attends a special school where she has a personalized curriculum to support her communication skills and her general education. Hayley has kindness as one of her strengths and she enjoys helping out in class and at home. Encouraging Hayley to assist with class routines gives her considerable satisfaction. She is aware that she finds learning difficult and can get extremely frustrated with her work. Nurturing Hayley's strength of kindness helps to counterbalance the frustration and draws her attention to the positive contribution she can make. Because Hayley can use her strength of kindness on a daily basis she regularly experiences the autonomy and competence this brings her.

## A personal strength brings meaning and satisfaction

A personal strength is something which we can perform well and with ease but is not necessarily a talent. The word talent identifies exceptional performance which is achieved by only a small percentage of the population. In contrast, a personal strength is something which meets our own needs. It is intrinsically motivating and is not dependent on external rewards or praise. A strength is something you would want to do whether or not you have an audience. Think of all the people who love to play an instrument although they would never win a talent contest. Using a strength leads to personal satisfaction which makes us want to use that skill again.

Strengths are part of a child's personal identity which will grow and change over the course of childhood. Some of the strengths which nourish us in childhood will fade away as interests change, while others will become stronger and more important. At each stage in a child's life their strengths are that dynamic part of themselves which provide energy, focus and satisfaction.

Childhood is a time of change and growth and we should not see it as a problem when one interest fades while others take over. It would be a mistake to anticipate too early what part any one strength may play in a child's life or to see these very personal explorations as something that will create a lifetime's purpose. Sometimes that does happen, but at other times children move on. As adults our role is to support and make things possible rather than to direct or try to hothouse any strength too intensively.

## IDENTIFYING PERSONAL STRENGTHS

### The 20 prime strengths

I have selected 20 strengths which each play a significant role in supporting a child's development and wellbeing as they mature towards adult life. While all 20 are positive qualities which are beneficial to any child, not all will be natural strengths for everyone. Some strengths will emerge with ease while others are a learned behaviour a child can perform with effort when the occasion demands it.

Table 1 lists the 20 prime strengths. It is divided into three sections, which identify personal strengths, learning strengths and social strengths. I have called these 20 key strengths 'prime strengths' because they form the important framework upon which children can build their personal identity.

Most of the research on identifying strengths has focused on adults. Psychologists have explored the variety of skills which are found in mature and competent adults. These strength descriptors acknowledge the diversity of skills that different people may bring to any situation. There are a number of published strengths tests which may identify up to 60 possible strengths. These tests are usually used in work settings to help people to identify their particular profile of strengths.

We need to take a different approach for children as their skills are emerging and liable to change over time. A guide to developing children's strengths needs to focus on supporting those core strengths which have universal value to children's development across childhood.

The 20 strengths selected as 'prime strengths' are drawn from highly respected strengths classifications. From those taxonomies of strengths I have included only those strengths which begin to emerge early in childhood. I am indebted to the work of Martin Seligman and Chris Petersen for their Values in Action Questionnaire[16] and to Alex Linley's Realise2.[17] I have also drawn upon Howard Gardner's Multiple Intelligences in the area of Learning Strengths.[18]

Prime strengths have the power to build a child's psychological wellbeing and start them off on a positive journey through childhood which will build their capacity to flourish.

## There is much more to strengths than good performance

Someone who has a musical strength may have to spend many hours in practice before they will achieve mastery of an instrument. The love of musical form and rhythm is the inner drive which persists through many long, dispiriting years of learning to play an instrument competently. The motivating role of strengths is vitally important to help us understand how strengths shape a child's life. Strengths influence our choices and drive us forward. When something is a strength we choose to use it and will do so without an audience or a reward. We do it for its own sake and when we do, it energizes us and absorbs our attention.

## Discovering and developing strengths

Strengths create a virtuous circle. Children discover that some things attract them more than others and that attraction grows as they achieve success and satisfaction. Children find their strengths attractive, not because they will be useful for ever but because they meet a need right now and do it in a playful way. Fun and play seem to have an evolutionary purpose, the pleasure we experience in play keeps us engaged and practising.

## The downside of modern childhood

We have not fully understood until recently how important it is to nurture children's strengths. In previous centuries each person, however young, contributed to their family and their community in the best way that they could. This was from necessity rather than from any understanding of the importance for children of being competent and involved.

Table 1: The 20 Prime Strengths

| Personal strengths | Each strength is a potential source of motivation which will influence a child's personal style of involvement with the world. |
| --- | --- |
| 1. Vitality/zest for life | Brings energy and excitement to most occasions and is outgoing and curious about people and activities |
| 2. Playfulness/humour | Can see the potential for fun and shares that with others |
| 3. Courage | Shows bravery in approaching new and challenging situations |
| 4. Perseverance/bounce back | Shows 'true grit' when the going gets tough |
| 5. Self-driven/improver | Is self-motivated and eager to find out ways to improve performance |
| 6. Composure/self-control | Able to control short-term feelings for long-term gain |
| 7. Hope/optimism | Views the future as full of possibilities |
| **Learning strengths** | These strengths identify the types of activity which attract attention and keep a child's interest. They are fulfilling and provide satisfaction. |
| 8. Practical/young scientist | Shows curiosity about both the natural and manmade world and is interested in things and how they work |
| 9. Creative | Uses imagination to explore new and different possibilities |
| 10. Musical | Drawn to rhythm and melody |
| 11. Adventure loving | Enjoys movement and physical challenge |
| 12. Love of language | Enjoys the sounds and rhythms of words and how they convey a message |
| **Social strengths** | These strengths are the personal values and beliefs which nurture relationships and allow them to flourish. |
| 13. Love and belonging | Has the ability to connect with others at a deep level |
| 14. Kindness/generosity | Takes care of others' needs in a practical way |
| 15. Honesty/genuineness | Remains true to personal values when doing so requires courage |
| 16. Fairness/justice | Stands up for what is good rather than what is easy |
| 17. Gratitude | Shows appreciation to others for their kindness and support |
| 18. Social sensitivity | Is quick to pick up cues about how others are feeling |
| 19. Communicator/listener | Connects well with others through language and ideas |
| 20. Leadership/inspiration | Works with others to motivate and guide their actions |

This necessity of working to help a family survive naturally allowed children to work with their strengths. Children's lives in pre-industrial societies may have been focused on survival and demanded relentless hard work but adults tended to build upon what a child brought to the task. This is the natural thing to do when working with a child and wanting them to learn quickly. Children's strengths in previous generations were acknowledged and given expression.

## How over-protection can suppress a child's strengths

As our world has become richer in resources, and less dependent on day to day survival, the need for children to work in the world's richest countries has been removed. The horrors of child labour during the industrial revolution reinforced the urge to protect children and to preserve childhood for as long as possible. We have an idealized image of childhood as a time of innocence, a space to be protected and cared for before we enter the hurly burly of life. This is an attractive image and is only possible because of our relative wealth. Our awareness of the harsh lives of children in the developing world increases our desire to protect our children.

## Avoiding a world of limits

However, for most children we have unintentionally created a world of limits. Those well-intentioned safety nets and protective actions have become constraints. We risk creating a gilded cage of childhood. In earlier centuries women were removed from the workforce as a sign of the family's relative wealth but often felt stifled and constrained. Now children are free to take time to grow and learn but do so at the cost of lost freedom and autonomy.

The protection, guidance and management we have built into children's lives have reduced their opportunities to experiment and find out what really excites and motivates them. Modern childhood risks being far more constrained than is good for children and that can lead to problems with children's behaviour and tensions in their relationships with adults.

## The impact of busy lives

Travelling to school by car is one example of how changes in lifestyle have had unintended consequences for children. Walking to school is now uncommon and the convenience of a car or bus journey is seen as an advantage. However, for previous generations, the walk to school and time in the playground before school started gave children time to be playful and relaxed. They arrived at school having let off some steam and maybe having practised some new skill like cartwheels or skipping which made them feel competent. Now car journeys are a source of stress for many families. Children dawdle in the morning, the family leaves late feeling stressed and arguments in the car just add to the agitation.

### Children need a new role

Our society has inadvertently left children with fewer outlets for the dynamic power that nature provides to ensure our survival. Children no longer need to work to help the family but their drive to develop their personal power and impact on the world has not been successfully re-routed elsewhere. While our world is undoubtedly safer and healthier, we have unintentionally lost sight of the paramount importance of building on the natural strengths each child brings to life and learning. I do believe this is a root cause of some behavioural problems that we commonly find.

### What has happened to children's behaviour?

In today's world, too often the power and energy children have, is either left idling, looking for a satisfying outlet or is organized by adults into structured activities where there is little room for children to do their own thing. A popular TV parenting programme recently suggested that on average children have only 49 minutes a day doing things with their parents.[19] This can leave children lacking the experience they need to explore and use their personal strengths. Difficult behaviour is a puzzle, which I believe we can understand better when we ask 'What would make this child happy?' and 'How can they learn to find autonomy and competence so that they can use their strengths creatively?'

## BUILDING AND USING PERSONAL STRENGTHS

### Nurturing self-discovery

Giving a child's inner motivation room to grow may be complicated by our security concerns and by how we educate children. We need to identify how to help children explore and feed their own curiosity. This is essential to the development of strengths. Children need to time to discover who they are, what they enjoy and to develop their strengths.

## BOX 4  TEN WAYS TO ENCOURAGE SELF-DISCOVERY LEARNING

1. Make sure there is enough spare time in the day so that children are not only free to choose but expected to entertain themselves.

2. If necessary identify ways to save time which then belongs to the child.

3. Provide a safe space and access to interesting toys and materials which will give them ideas for creative and imaginative play. It can be difficult at first for children unused to free time to rely on their imagination but this will improve with practice.

4. Creativity thrives on freedom. Less is more in the toy department if you want children to reach inside themselves for ideas and motivation.

5. Consider rotating toys and equipment so children are not overwhelmed by choice or tempted to flit between games without completing anything.

6. Make sure time available is uninterrupted; children often get absorbed in free play in the mornings and drive parents to distraction by being unwilling to stop. If time is limited, make the stop time crystal clear and for younger children use a kitchen timer.

7. Don't be tempted to ask for a report as this may make children feel obliged to get results rather than explore and experiment. A happy and fulfilled child will want to tell you but not all play gets big impact results.

8. Avoid TV and computer time clashing with self-discovery play. Both are passive, easy fixes for a tired child.

9. Separate social play with other children from self-discovery play which is independent. All children need to have both but learning about your strengths depends on the freedom to explore, which may not always be compatible with cooperative play with friends.

10. Look out for signs that a child is not having enough self-discovery play. Disputes with peers and lack of interest in an adult-led activity may be signs that the child needs a different balance between formal learning, cooperative play and self-discovery learning.

## How can schools nurture individual strengths?

When children are reluctant learners, and become withdrawn or disruptive, the pressure mounts to get children back on track. This can become a negative cycle, with the teacher overseeing more of what the child does and the child's opportunities to feel competent and in control shrinking further.

Many of the behaviour problems I meet in schools stem from children's need to escape a situation where they feel neither capable nor able to have any say in what happens. They start to do things that distract them from this gnawing dissatisfaction and search for things which bring at least a little fun and excitement. This is described as disruptive behaviour by schools, because the child is not seen as having any significant personal or emotional problems which might explain their actions. Teachers often look for triggers which might explain what sparked the behaviour. Anyone following a behaviourist approach assumes that the environment is the main influence on behaviour. They are puzzled by the lack of obvious triggers to explain what sparked the behaviour. However, the cause may be linked to how the child is feeling inside when their drive to succeed is compromised.

Increasingly schools are exploring how to create a learning environment which balances excellence in teaching while also ensuring high performance and supporting each student's need for competence and autonomy. The strengths movement in schools has been gaining ground particularly in the United States.[20]

## Discovering and developing prime strengths

Each of the 20 prime strengths outlined in Table 1 will build a child's wellbeing when it is voluntary but if using a strength becomes forced and directed by adults there is a risk of undermining the genuineness and spontaneity which nourishes each strength. We will look later at the difference between strengths and learned behaviours. Figure 1 illustrates how energy and performance interact to create prime strengths.

| High energy | Low energy |
|---|---|
| Undeveloped strengths <br> • child shows interest <br> • unrecognized by others <br> • underused or limited outlets <br> Low performance | Prime strengths <br> • energizing <br> • self-motivated <br> • used frequently <br> • personal best performance <br> • satisfying <br> High performance |
| Weaknesses <br> • low motivation <br> • weak personal performance <br> • draining emotionally <br> • avoids or performs under pressure <br> Low performance | Learned behaviour <br> • high performance <br> • required or demanded by others <br> • emotionally draining <br> • rarely spontaneous <br> High performance |

Figure 1   How energy and performance levels interact to create prime strengths
*Source:* adapted from Linley, Willars and Biswas-Diener 2010.[21]

## How to identify prime strengths

Observing what children do and how they do it is the best way to identify prime strengths.

We are looking for what is motivating and energizing for the child rather than rating the level of performance. We have all met children who have a natural skill but little enthusiasm for using it. Every dance class, sporting event and music school has young children brought along by their parents who are hoping their child will do well.

I have no problems in principle with learning skills that are useful, we all have to do that in all areas of our lives. These skills are described as learned behaviour by Alex Linley, the author of the Realise2 strengths profile, which is well established in the business sector. He stresses the importance of identifying when people are high performers, but not inspired by using their skill. This is vital to avoid having to over-use a learned behaviour because of the draining effect of high effort with low satisfaction. This can lead to burnout.

We see burnout in child prodigies whose parents have had more enthusiasm than their child. A talent is not necessarily a strength unless it becomes a core part of our personal identity. The test between a talent and a strength is whether someone would they describe themselves as a musician or as someone who plays the violin at Grade VI? We choose our strengths. Working long hours to practise a skill is not a problem when you are passionate about what you are doing but is stressful and draining if it isn't intrinsically satisfying.

To identify when something is a strength look out for the signs that show a strength in action.

## BOX 5   SEVEN SIGNPOSTS OF PRIME STRENGTHS

### 1. Energy and enthusiasm

- Notice the positive energy in both movement and speech.
- Are movements lively and energetic?
- Is posture relaxed and open?
- Is language positively phrased?
- Is the tone of voice lively?
- Is there a playful quality?

### 2. Persistence and effort

- Is mastering the next step approached with a lively curiosity?
- Does time fly by when absorbed in practice?
- Do you have to give a five-minute warning to get them to stop?

### 3. Making it look easy

- Are children fluent and accurate in what they are doing so that the skill appears effortless?
- Do they have more stamina when using this strength than is usual?

### 4. Attention and engagement

- Can children shut out the world around them when using this strength?
- Is careful attention paid to getting details correct?

### 5. Speed of learning

- Does a child make rapid progress with minimal support?
- Does the child find it easy to identify how different elements of the skill fit together?
- Can they easily transfer what they have learned to a new situation?

### 6. Willingness to take on a challenge

- When what they are doing becomes complex do they rise to the challenge independently?

### 7. Eagerness to problem solve

- If they do need help are they eager to seek it out and to learn from someone else?
- Are they excited by solving the problem and moving on?

These seven steps describe a very motivated, self-directed learner. But don't despair if you find a child is not like that a lot of the time. Strengths do not emerge fully formed and need time and opportunities to grow and develop. The Prime Strengths Finder on the following page can be used to consider a child's strengths. It is not designed as a 'to do list'. Don't expect every child to tick all the boxes. It is intended to help you explore what comes naturally for a child so you can help them make more of that strength knowing that this will give them natural satisfaction.

The completed Prime Strengths Finder identifies strengths in action through frequency of use, energy level (and enthusiasm) and ease of performance. This gives you an overview of a child's strengths, learned behaviours and weaknesses. Although we may be tempted to focus on weaknesses this is not going to energise children or give them confidence. Supporting children to make optimal use of their strengths should start with what matters most to them. Focusing attention on the top three strengths is a good starting point. Do ask children what they think. Young children may find this difficult at first, but with your help to increase their self-awareness they will find it easier to make good choices in how they use their time productively.

# Prime Strengths Finder

| Strength | Frequency of use | High energy level | Performs with ease |
|---|---|---|---|
| **Personal strengths** | | | |
| 1. Vitality/zest for life | | | |
| 2. Playfulness/humour | | | |
| 3. Courage | | | |
| 4. Perseverance/bounce back | | | |
| 5. Self-driven/improver | | | |
| 6. Composure/self-control | | | |
| 7. Hope/optimism | | | |
| **Learning strengths** | | | |
| 8. Practical/young scientist | | | |
| 9. Creative | | | |
| 10. Musical | | | |
| 11. Adventure loving | | | |
| 12. Love of language | | | |
| **Social strengths** | | | |
| 13. Love and belonging | | | |
| 14. Kindness/generosity | | | |
| 15. Honesty/genuineness | | | |
| 16. Fairness/justice | | | |
| 17. Gratitude | | | |
| 18. Social sensitivity | | | |
| 19. Communicator/listener | | | |
| 20. Leadership/inspiration | | | |

✓

# Top Three Prime Strengths

| Prime strength | What happens now | New opportunities |
| --- | --- | --- |
| 1. | | |
| 2. | | |
| 3. | | |

✓

When you identify areas where a child is showing a definite preference you can consider how to create more opportunities to use this strength. Does the child's day have a good balance of using strengths alongside learning new skills?

Children spend a lot of time learning new skills at school which they struggle to master; this may leave them feeling frustrated and incompetent. Children spend on average more time doing things they don't find easy than most adults do. This can be frustrating and, as a child's emotions are still maturing, it can expose them to pressure they don't yet have the skills to manage. Finding a child's strengths and creating opportunities for them to use these strengths to good effect builds confidence as well as bringing success.

## Why build strengths?

If strengths are personal choices which children use spontaneously, shouldn't we just get out of the way and see what happens? It is definitely true that children need more personal space but they also have less control over their lives. We need to reduce the barriers which set limits to children being able to discover and use their strengths. Children need planned adult support to create the right conditions for strengths to grow.

### BOX 6   TEN WAYS TO HELP CHILDREN BUILD THEIR STRENGTHS

1.  Free up at least an hour a day for free play to give children time to explore and develop their strengths independently.

2.  Notice what is done with enthusiasm and relish and then praise that willingness and effort. Focus on the process not the result.

3.  Share your passions and what motivates you so children can experience another perspective and compare their interests with other people's.

4.  Talk about things that you enjoyed at the same age and why it mattered to you. Help the child find out about what worked for other people too. This encourages a sense of individuality and diversity.

5.  Have toys and materials available which support a particular strength.

6.  Borrow and make things together which can form part of the creative resources available for further exploration and play.

7. Introduce stories, DVDs, games and opportunities to role play so that a prime strength can be explored and used imaginatively.

8. Give positive feedback to ensure that the child's efforts are noticed and valued.

9. Find out what you can about others who share that strength and who may be useful role models.

10. Create opportunities for children to volunteer to use their strength but don't create pressure to perform.

## Discovering undeveloped strengths

Don't despair if you find a child isn't firing on all cylinders. Instead use the statements in the seven signposts checklist and reverse the questions from positive statements to ask 'What would it take to help this child feel this way?' You will be looking for undeveloped strengths which may need your help to find an outlet.

## Where to look

Children tend to use their strengths naturally in their free play. Ensuring that a child has at least an hour a day of uninterrupted time to do as they choose should encourage a child to explore and experiment. Listen out for what they tell you about their play and where the energy and enthusiasm pinpoints a possible strength.

## Choose the smallest thing you can do that will make the biggest difference?

Igniting the spark to help a strength to grow is a subtle process, more of a slow burn than a massive blaze which has been artificially fuelled and quickly burns out. Aim to help children discover their strengths under their own steam by creating the opportunities rather than actively teaching or tutoring. As children mature over the years their interests grow and change. An interest in making sledges and go-carts, for the sheer thrill of not only going faster but doing so under your own steam, can be a childhood strength that can develop in any number of ways. If we are to nurture children's dynamic drive to explore and learn we adults have to take a back seat. We can rarely second guess what might happen next.

## *Encourage competence and autonomy*

The most important lesson for life for any child is that sense of self-determination: 'I did that,' 'I made it happen.' The more opportunities children have to get involved with an activity that gives them satisfaction, the more motivated they become.

## SUMMARY

- A strength is a source of personal power and motivation which brings meaning and satisfaction to a child's life.

- Self Determination Theory reminds us that people flourish when they have autonomy, a sense of competence and strong relationships.

- Children may have fewer opportunities and outlets to discover and use their strengths than is beneficial for their wellbeing.

- Emotional and behavioural difficulties may result from the more limited opportunities available to this generation to develop autonomy and competence.

- Self-discovery learning is an essential part of developing a strong personal identity and self-esteem.

- There are 20 prime strengths which are developmentally important to children.

- Prime strengths can be identified and nurtured using the seven signposts which characterize strength-based behaviour.

- Strengths are energizing and fulfilling so children will benefit from using their top three strengths daily.

Factor 2

# Emotional Wellbeing
## Creating a Positive Balance

### Overview

Discover:

- how emotional wellbeing underpins personal, social and learning success
- why early experiences provide a secure base for all aspects of development
- ways to nurture emotional security to rebalance an unsettled start
- how to boost the energy and enthusiasm children need for exploration and learning
- how to support the development of emotional competence
- how to help a child create a positive balance of emotions.

## UNDERSTANDING EMOTIONAL WELLBEING

Emotional wellbeing is not the same as happiness. Creating emotional wellbeing depends on more than increasing the episodes of happiness we experience across the day. Wellbeing results from the ability to manage emotions.

Emotional wellbeing can be described as:

*Having the energy and enthusiasm for life and the self-control and motivation to pursue worthwhile goals.*

Our emotions evolved to alert us to anything in the world around us that might help or hinder our day to day survival. At the beginning of childhood a baby can only respond passively to what happens and has no control over their environment. Wellbeing is affected by how well we learn to integrate emotional experience with rational thought to make choices which suit us and make good use of our strengths and experience.

There are three aspects of emotional development which together create wellbeing:

1. Becoming securely bonded with family to feel protected and supported.

2. Developing emotional self-awareness and competence to manage both your own emotions and your relationship with others successfully.

3. The ability to manage the 'negativity bias' created by our protective emotions to create a positive balance of emotions.

## What emotions do for us

All emotions serve a useful purpose and contribute to our survival. We repress or ignore them at our peril. Some emotions serve to push us away from potential harm, while others signal that all is well and leave us free to focus on activities which contribute positively to our lives.

The number of emotions which exist to protect us from harm outnumber the positive emotions which attract us to enjoyable experiences. While this was undoubtedly useful for survival, it now makes it vitally necessary for family and community to stoke up the positive emotions in a child's life and reduce the negatives. This needs to happen in a healthy way that goes deeper than physical pleasures such as eating and drinking. Gradually children learn to make choices for themselves based on what they have learned from adult guidance.

Defining the different emotions is not a simple task. The vocabulary of emotion words is huge and the subtle variations in shades of meaning have made it difficult for scientists to agree precise labels and to decide which emotions are primary and which secondary.

The eight emotions discussed below are widely accepted as the primary emotions.

### 1. ANGER

Anger is a powerful reaction to a perceived threat. Its evolutionary value is the creation of energy to protect you from harm. It releases adrenaline which speeds up the flow of blood to the muscles in preparation for a fight. However, it is also a sign of insecurity and shows that you feel something is about to undermine the world you live in and leave you seriously harmed. Other emotions in the anger family include annoyance, irritability, resentment, hostility, vexation, exasperation, hatred and outrage.

## Managing anger

Low-level general stress raises the bar for reacting angrily. It can trigger the full anger response at a much lower level than normal, for example, when queuing or when stuck in traffic. Reducing general stress and raising positive experiences will both reduce the frequency and intensity of angry responses.

Slowing down the pace of life and actively including enjoyable experiences reduces the risk of over-reacting to anger-inducing experiences. Taking stock of the environmental pressures on a child is a first step to anger management. Anger is a response to a perceived threat which needs to be understood and problem solved. Behaviour coaching is a valuable approach to helping children understand their feelings and seek solutions, and is described in detail later.

## 2. FEAR

Fear is the equal but opposite reaction to anger but now the threat seems frightening and insurmountable. If children do not believe they can fight back, fear usually leads to avoidance or to a passive response. Avoiding something that creates fear means that children will not find out whether the feared object would have harmed them or whether they could have done anything to overcome it. Fear is therefore a very resistant emotion once it takes hold. Related emotions include wariness, anxiety, nervousness, dread and terror.

## Managing fear

Children need to know that the feared object cannot harm them. This will require slow and sensitive exposure to the feared object. It is important that the adult shows no fear but accepts that the child's feelings are genuine and not to be dismissed. This will help the child's fears to gradually reduce. Anxieties and fears in childhood are commonplace and reflect the vulnerability and limited control a child has in their life at this point. Mastering fears give children confidence in themselves which is why scary stories or fairground rides are so enjoyable.

## 3. SADNESS

Sadness is a reaction to loss which is designed to protect you from further harm. It works by slowing us down and taking us out of the action. In earlier times sadness may have created an acceptance of defeat in battle and given the injured person time to recover. More usually, now, sadness is linked to personal separation and loss. Grief produces severe emotional pain which needs time for mourning and recovery. Sadness is in essence linked to a loss of control and when this helplessness becomes pervasive it can lead to depression. Related feelings include grief, sorrow, loneliness, despair and melancholy.

### Coping with sadness

Sadness needs time and a safe, supportive environment for natural healing to take place. People can be uncomfortable with a child's sadness and can set unrealistic expectations about bouncing back from grief and loss. For children experiencing parental separation it can be particularly difficult to mourn the loss of the intact family life as well as the loss of the parent who no longer lives with them. Sadness which is not given an outlet or a means of control can deepen into depression.

## 4. ENJOYMENT

Enjoyment is an energizing emotion which responds to our sense that all is well in the world. Pleasure gives us that lift which encourages us to engage in something productive. Related emotions include happiness, joy, contentment, delight and rapture. Short-term enjoyment is found in eating and drinking but this is short lived. Having an enjoyable experience has a long-lasting effect, so a day out or a visit to the theatre or cinema has more impact than eating ice cream. Children and families who over-eat, often lead restricted lives and are encouraged to get out together not only for the exercise but also for the lifting effect on mood.[22]

### Creating enjoyment

Community events create enjoyment and build bonds between people. Community projects are being grant aided to build community links. For many people enjoyment has become a more solitary pursuit. When people are isolated from each other rates of depression are greater. Shared activities build and sustain social bonds and are an important part of building any community. Schools focus on sports, arts and drama to create a strong sense of shared purpose. The strengths-based schools movement actively encourages communal action including story telling and community celebrations to build both individual and community identity through a focus on strengths.[23]

## 5. LOVE

Love is the intense and sustained emotion which creates a close bond between partners, families and friends. It creates a desire to care for that person and be loved in return. Love builds the closeness and intimacy required for interdependent relationships and softens our reactions to any competing needs or viewpoints. Love is an enabler that creates tolerance, acceptance and loyalty. In the love family of feelings are friendliness, devotion and adoration.

### Sustaining love

Love is a two-way relationship built on give and take. Love is built on actions more than words. We explore how parental attunement and sensitivity to a child's needs nurtures a child's development in more detail later. Losing the love of another person is deeply traumatic and children frequently check out that they are loved and valued. The term 'attention seeking' is an unhelpful way of interpreting this natural behaviour.

## 6. SURPRISE

Surprise is a valuable emotion; it ensures we do not become complacent in our surroundings and that we notice any changes which might be detrimental. It explains why the fun surprises which family and friends create for us can be a mixture of pleasure and unease. Small children don't always take to surprises and can disappoint the person who planned it by being shocked and upset rather than overjoyed. Surprise does seem to have a close link to the anxious/fear response. Here we can also include shock, astonishment, amazement and wonder.

### Surprise and managing change

For young children, at the stage before language skills develop, routine is important to help make sense of the world. Unpredictability is unsettling and can make the world seem unsafe. Surprises are delightful when they bring us something valuable but unexpected.

## 7. DISGUST

Disgust protects us from anything that may be physically harmful and make us ill. Certain strong smells are particularly disgusting and are often linked to decomposition and decay.

### Dealing with disgust

Children have a powerful disgust response which is protective and dissuades them from touching or eating anything harmful when they are small. However, they do need time to build their familiarity with different foods and can react with disgust if they encounter something new. Contempt, disdain, scorn, abhorrence, aversion, distaste and revulsion are also close relatives.

## 8. SHAME

Shame, like enjoyment is a social emotion which maintains communities. Shame is an important response to social disapproval which protects children by making sure they stop the behaviour which gets this response. Shame develops in early childhood in response to those who love and care for us and is a reaction which helps to maintain the close bond as the child becomes more active, independent and at risk of danger. Guilt, embarrassment, remorse, humiliation, regret and contrition also belong in this family.

### The role of shame

Shame can act as a useful reminder that a behaviour has created disapproval. When over-used it can be humiliating and creates a sense of rejection which can push a child beyond the bonds that bind a group. Where love has been in short supply, shame is likely to be diminished because the unsupported child has had to learn to depend on their own instincts and has not been able to trust others to care for them. Building trust and establishing a loving relationship paradoxically renews a child's capacity to feel shame. Shame is a much misunderstood emotion and if we discourage it we risk encouraging people to be self-centred and lacking in empathy.

These eight emotions have a powerful role in regulating behaviour. The negative emotions warn us of potential dangers while the positive emotions energise us and help sustain our efforts to learn and grow. The protective emotions outnumber the positive emotions, creating a negativity bias which can impact on psychological wellbeing. We will explore how emotional wellbeing can be built and boosted in everyday life.

# EMOTIONAL LEARNING AND WELLBEING

When children know adults will provide for them and protect them they feel secure, and their negative emotions become less frequent and intense. A child will be less preoccupied with their own inner turmoil and can look around to discover the world and the people in it. They can focus attention outwards rather than engage with the insistent demands of the emotional brain. A calmer, happier child is free to learn.

## Emotional learning and security

Emotions guide us in making decisions which are too important to leave to intellect alone. We talk of our 'gut feeling' as providing an initial guide to making difficult decisions. We then back up these feelings with conscious thought to weigh up the various possibilities.

This may seem counterintuitive, and goes against the popular belief that intuition is to be mistrusted. However, scientists working with people who have had head injuries to parts of the brain involved in managing emotions have noted that this affects the ability to make decisions. They veer back and forth between various options with no emotional compass to guide them in what feels right for them. Dr Antonio Damasio, a cognitive neuroscientist, suggests their decision making deteriorates because they have lost access to their emotional learning.[24]

Emotional learning captures the important moments of life experience and helps us to decide what feels right. Emotional learning is stored as unconscious memories which we are not aware of but which remind us via 'gut reactions' what has worked or not worked for us in the past. Emotions guide decision making, and without an emotional steer we are unsure what to do.

## Emotional memories guide our decisions

Emotional learning begins in early childhood and is a vital component of wellbeing. However, it is not easy for us to examine because emotional memories are stored in a part of the brain not involved with language which makes them inaccessible to our conscious minds. Sigmund Freud was aware of the importance of emotional learning but he assumed these memories were deliberately repressed.[25] We now know that early emotional learning is stored in a different part of the brain called the limbic system. It is out of conscious awareness because it works differently, not because it has been repressed.

The emotional brain exists to keep a child safe. It is a relatively unsophisticated part of the brain which identifies potential threats and keeps this information in store so that if something similar happens again a fast reaction can be organized by matching the previous sensory pattern to the new one. In this simple form of perceptual pattern matching, sounds, smells, images and other sensations are stored away for future reference. Do you smell burning: is this an emergency? Is that barking sound linked to the big black creature which scared you the other day?

When emotional learning has been positive it boosts wellbeing and these unconsciously stored patterns help a child stay calm and optimistic in new situations. However, when life has been unsettled, a child's emotional learning is highly sensitized to possible threats. Children are likely to misread situations as threatening which then results in emotional over-arousal and behaviour difficulties.

Developing the ability to manage emotional wellbeing independently is a slow process which develops across the whole of childhood and adolescence. A child's emotional wellbeing is highly dependent on skilled adult support to help the child learn to be in control of their feelings rather than be controlled by them.

The brain is a complex system of many parts but is often described as having three functional areas:

1. *The brain stem*, which manages instinctual processes such as breathing, circulation, temperature control, digestion, balance.

2. *The emotional brain or limbic system*, which triggers strong emotions and works with the brain stem to activate flight or fight reflexes.

3. *The rational brain or cortex*, the higher brain responsible for all thought and reflection. It is the largest part of the brain, estimated at around 85 per cent of brain mass. This is the seat of self-awareness, creativity and active problem solving. Eventually our personal memories and all our formal learning will depend upon this part of the brain. When a child is born the brain cells in the cortex are abundant but no connections have yet been made.

The brain stem and the limbic system are well developed at birth, but the cortex depends on experience and learning to gain full capacity. The thinking brain takes time to mature and needs to be in a calm and attentive state to work well. The emotional brain can over-ride the cortex and a perceived threat seriously interferes with the process of learning.

## Understanding the emotional brain

The emotions are based deep in the brain, in the limbic system, which evolved before the cortex where language and thought are managed. Emotional perceptions are rapid and powerful. Messages to the emotional brain are quickly processed way ahead of the rational part of the brain which works slowly to weigh everything up and come to a decision. We can 'sense' danger long before we 'know' what has happened. If you are a driver or a cyclist you know how important this rapid response system is to our survival. We instantly react to a potentially dangerous situation without fully being aware of the details.

We need to understand and manage our emotions precisely because they are fast movers and will run away with us if left to themselves. Emotions are far from accurate judges of a situation; they jump to conclusions on very little evidence. Their speed is possible because of rapid pattern recognition: 'This is like the time when…' The startle reaction is a good example of the emotional brain at work. When we are feeling a bit stressed we are more likely to jump when we hear a noise or imagine there is something lurking in the shadows on a dark night.

Early fears and disappointments will become firmly embedded, creating the patterns which trip the emotional alarm system. Because they are both fast acting and happening outside conscious awareness this can lead to an emotional hijack each time something vaguely similar to a past threat occurs.

Learning to counterbalance emotional reactions with considered thought is one of the key tasks of childhood, to be able to manage the irrational fears stoked up by the trigger-happy limbic system. However, we need to be careful not to go the route of previous generations who mistrusted emotions completely and tried to ignore them. What we need is a unity of the three parts of the brain.

## Childhood experience determines how well the three brain regions work together

The emotional brain is highly sensitive in children and easily becomes over-aroused. Some children are never at peace; frequently at the mercy of primitive urges to attack or defend until they become ruled by pervasive anxiety or powerful, unresolved anger. They have not yet experienced the support they need to feel safe and secure.

Other children experience their distress as something to be avoided at all costs, so they grow up dissociated from all emotions, including love and joy, to live a life of over-rational control. Safe but emotionally stunted. They have been strongly persuaded not to make a fuss as it might make things worse. Adults who react strongly to a child's emotions can make the experience of being upset an anxious or frightening experience which the child learns to avoid.

The lucky ones have been helped to recognize when they need support, to resolve the problem and feel better. They understand how the rational brain can coordinate their reactions and are fortunate to have social awareness, compassion and intimacy working well in their lives.

## The role of the emotional brain

One of the problems with emotional memory is its persistence, unlike other memories they are remarkably resilient and don't easily get forgotten. The emotional memory area is linked to motor learning which needs to be permanent. If we easily lost motor memories we would forget how to walk or ride a bike, which would have dangerous consequences. So although you may forget a phone number you used yesterday, the slightest hint of something that made you cry years ago can catch you unawares with an upsurge of long forgotten feelings.

When children have a vast store of emotional memories linked to an insecure life, they will continue to react powerfully to any perceived threats. They have become sensitized to danger and need to overlay those images with a host of positive, safe and calming ones which can reset their emotional thermostat.

There has been an interest in early childhood experience and its lasting impact since Freud started writing about repressed memories. We will explore what creates security for children and how to use this knowledge to support children who are emotionally vulnerable.

## How emotional security is learned

Babies are born helpless and totally dependent on adult care; without that sensitive support a child could not survive. The baby's powerful cries are designed to draw attention to their needs, as well as to exercise their lungs. Their wellbeing depends on care; the baby cannot soothe or switch off their feelings by themselves and can only become calm again with adult help.

A calm and reassuring parent gradually soothes and reassures the child. Emotional wellbeing starts from this early, secure care which minimizes distress and helps the baby to quickly return to a calm state. The baby depends on the adult to tune in to their feelings and needs a parent who can cope with the heavy demands of parenting without being overwhelmed by their own competing emotional demands. An emotionally absent or inconsistent carer leaves the baby in an over-aroused state for long periods.

Babies can recognize and respond to an adult's expression. A calm and reassuring parent gradually calms and reassures the child. An anxious or angry carer may feed or change a child, but not soothe their feelings adequately, leaving them anxious and easily upset.

Children depend on their parents to understand and interpret their needs. A strong bond between mother and child creates sensitivity to the child's needs so that any distress is quickly picked up on and addressed. This support helps the child to rapidly recover from distress and become secure knowing that they will be looked after. Attuned parenting also demonstrates soothing actions which the child gradually copies, so they learn to calm themselves when the parent isn't there.

Gradually, as a result of their experience, the child builds an 'internal working model of the world'[26] which helps them to predict how adults react. Although a baby is physically weak and helpless they have a remarkable ability to sense whether an adult's reactions are hostile or supportive.

Where the child's main care giver is responsive and available, the child anticipates care and enjoys their carer's company. The child learns that when they smile or laugh this will attract the adult to play and that crying when hungry or uncomfortable will bring care. The child's needs are promptly met and the child remains happy and calm.

## Distress and the emotional brain

Children who are emotionally secure typically calm down quickly and resume their play. Exactly how this more rapid calming process develops between mother and child has been studied in detail by filming mother/child interactions. Mothers who are attuned to their babies needs communicate that they have understood what the child is feeling. When the child is cooing and happy, the mother responds with her own delight and a reciprocal dance of pleasure is playfully communicated between them. If the child is in distress, then the mother will give comfort and by slowing the pace of her response will settle and soothe her child. Whether the child's emotions are joyful or sad the mother demonstrates an understanding and a practical response which works with the child's feelings. The pace and the pattern are determined by each micro-reaction from the child.

From this experience children learn three important lessons:

1. to recognize their own feelings from seeing what is reflected back to them

2. to trust that their mother can accept whatever they are feeling in a calm manner

3. to rely on their mother to respond to what they are communicating appropriately.

## The past need not decide the future

We have explored the importance of early emotional learning in shaping a child's wellbeing, but this does not assume a life sentence for children and families where there have been difficulties.

Human beings have an amazing capacity for change. Although early experience has a major impact on the developing brain, the brain is adaptable, with so-called neuroplasticity, which allows the brain to learn from new experience. Good experiences will gradually over-ride the negative. Children can make new relationships that help them to thrive. Parents can be helped to repair family relationships when they receive support which models the sensitivity and rapport which characterizes positive relationships. It is never too late to form a new working model of the world.

## Exploring and understanding a child's emotional security

When children are often fearful, anxious or emotionally volatile this is a clear indication that they are struggling to feel safe and calm. Less obvious signs of emotional vulnerability can be children who avoid new experiences or who are reluctant to take risks or make mistakes.

Children who are emotionally secure are more able to seek adult support. They can respond to opportunities to join an activity which will distract them from their feelings and are able to participate in something which they can enjoy. Emotionally insecure children are more likely to become 'stuck' in an emotional state and find it hard to regulate their feelings and move on. Building a supportive relationship can take time.

## BOX 7  TEN WAYS TO BUILD A CHILD'S TRUST AND SOOTHE TROUBLED FEELINGS

1. Let children know you have recognized that they are upset and that you can accept how they are feeling. Give reassurance through body language and voice tone as well as what you say.

2. Help children to recognize what they are feeling without guilt or expectations of reprisal. Name what they may be feeling: 'I think you are feeling angry.'

3. Communicate that you are willing to help them to resolve their distress and support them during this process.

4. Create a safe space for the child to regain calm. Offer adult support or calming activities to help reduce the physiological arousal.

5. Give a clear message that powerful feelings are not punished or rejected but destructive behaviour is not acceptable.

6. When the child has recovered from the initial upset, explore what has happened and discuss how the child could have reacted differently.

7. Ensure a vulnerable child is regularly reminded of their strengths and is encouraged to value themselves. Suggest that the child uses a strength as a distraction or to resolve an issue.

8. Make sure the child has a strong sense of belonging and need not fear rejection. When children are upset, let them know you want to help them feel better, but make sure they do not feel that their upset is inconvenient or unacceptable to you. Some children who are insecure believe they are only acceptable to others when they are doing well.

9. Create opportunities to build and reinforce the child's relationships with adults and peers. Helping and sharing reinforces mutual dependency. Give and take, or reciprocity, is a strong foundation for feeling good about yourself because others demonstrate that they respect, value and care for you. The bigger the child's community, the more secure they can become. Many emotionally vulnerable children become at risk of social exclusion from their peer group unless they are helped to be fully included.

10. Don't be discouraged by the slow pace of change. Be aware that a child who expects rejection may be slow to develop trust. Their mistrust may create a protective barrier which keeps people at a distance.

We will explore how children develop mastery over their emotions in the next section.

## UNDERSTANDING AND NURTURING EMOTIONAL COMPETENCE

Children need to learn to recognize and understand their emotions so they can gain control over what the emotional brain is telling them. Emotional competence is the ability to be aware of feelings but also to take account of what you think before you decide on a course of action. The emotional brain is powerful and learning to manage it is a major life achievement. Learning to coordinate the emotional and the rational brain has been compared with learning to ride an elephant.[27] Humans may try to plan where they wish to go but the animal beneath is hugely strong and powerful and not totally predictable.

There are five skills which children need to manage their emotional wellbeing:

1. *Recognizing their emotions:* being able to monitor their feelings from moment to moment allows them to decide what to do.

2. *Managing emotions:* being able to self-regulate strong feelings avoids them being at the mercy of powerful emotions which can undermine what they set out to do.

3. *Self-motivation:* managing the conflict between what seems attractive in the short term in order to work towards longer-term goals. Resisting the power of emotional impulses requires considerable self-discipline and restraint.

4. *Recognizing emotions in others:* empathy allows them to recognize what others may be feeling and theory of mind allows them to separate their feelings and needs from their own.

5. *Developing and maintaining relationships:* the art of relationships depends upon sensitivity to the needs of others and fluent social skills to build rapport and trust.

These five skill areas develop gradually over the course of a lifetime. Some people learn to ride the elephant while others have only limited control. Developing emotional competence is rarely achieved without sensitive adult support. We will now explore how adults can help children understand and manage their emotions.

## 1. Recognizing their emotions

Children are particularly at the mercy of powerful emotions; their vulnerability and need for protection is acknowledged by nature which provides them with super-strength emotional reactions, which alert the child to potential danger and also makes sure that any nearby adult can't ignore the fact either. This reaction is called attachment behaviour, designed to protect children and keep adults tuned in to ensure children are safe. Attachment behaviour persists throughout childhood but becomes more muted as young people gain confidence in their ability to handle situations by themselves or with the help of friends.

Babies first become aware of their feelings when they are reflected back to them. A smiling child who is smiled at in return and who senses matched body language and tone of voice begins to recognize enjoyment. An anxious baby becomes soothed by the reassurance shown to them which recognizes their anxiety and holds them safe from it. The synchrony between child and carer mirrors and matches the child's feelings and allows the child to recognize what is happening. Later the words being used add meaning and the language of emotion is shared.

## 2. Managing emotions

When children are engulfed by their emotions they cannot stand back from them and need an adult to provide reassurance and practical support to:

- help them feel safe and protected from harm even if objectively there is no threat
- build trust that the adult will be consistent and reliable in helping them manage strong feelings
- reduce the over-aroused physiological state which accelerates the flight or fight response
- teach children the language to recognize and label this pattern of feeling.

### ANNIE'S STORY

Annie was a very anxious, quiet child who had experienced a lot of upheaval in her life. The family had moved twice in her first two years at school and these changes of school had proved unsettling. Annie's education had also been disrupted and there were gaps in her knowledge. When faced with something new, she tended to freeze, and could not get started. Tania, the teaching assistant, was able to build her relationship with Annie, sitting quietly beside her at times when the class teacher was introducing a new theme. Tania found that a gentle, soothing approach was calming for Annie. She would catch Annie's eye and smile at her. She avoided telling her she knew she could do it as Annie's body language said the complete opposite. Instead she would say, 'Come and see me if you need help.' Over time Annie took up her offer less and less often. In time their smiles at each other became more signs of anticipation rather than exchanges of reassurance. Annie felt that Tania understood her, did not judge her and would help if needed. This was just what she was looking for.

## LEARNING TO MANAGE FEELINGS

Children's behaviour is often problematic because they are trying to solve a problem of their own. Learning to understand your emotions takes time and often a child's solution is both impulsive and centred on their own needs. They are not trying to create a problem for others but often this is just what happens. To learn to understand themselves and others better, children need sensitive guidance which helps them to look at every aspect of their behaviour and find a better solution. I call this behaviour coaching, which is designed to work from the outside in, teaching a child to recognize the thoughts and feelings which contribute to their behaviour. Behaviour coaching may appear to take longer than offering a quick solution of your own, but it is more effective in calming the situation. It also gradually teaches the child how to find their own solutions. Empathy is at the heart of this approach. When you acknowledge, and try to understand the child's feelings, you will help them to make sense of their own emotions. It will then be easier to find solutions which work for the child.

There are five stages to take you from acknowledging the problem to finding a solution. Behaviour coaching helps a child learn how to integrate the emotional brain with rational thought. Behaviour coaching is designed to identify and acknowledge the child's feelings and how they impact on behaviour. When this has been successful you can help the child identify what new behaviours and skills need to be learned and practised.

Your empathy provides a close connection with the child, and improves communication so that you can both explore what has happened and why the child is feeling this way. It helps reduce stress and makes thinking and reflection easier.

It is a vital principle of all coaching that the coach does not advise or direct. You may see a solution, but what you are aiming for is to help the child understand themselves better. Then they can make informed choices and plan genuine change. When you talk to a child about their feelings keep your views private to avoid inhibiting the child from finding what works for them. While being given a solution may be a quick fix, it doesn't teach the child how to think through and solve problems for themselves.

## MONITOR YOUR OWN FEELINGS

It is also important to be aware of how you feel about powerful emotions. Your empathy and connection with a child will be affected by your own values and beliefs about strong feelings. Do you avoid sadness or perhaps you fear anger? It is not unusual to 'catch an emotion' when someone is upset and feel something of the same strong emotions that the child is feeling. If you are uncomfortable with any of these feelings, you are more likely to try to resolve things quickly to restore your own peace of mind. Equally, barriers to communication can be created if someone piles on the guilt or creates shame in the hope this will prevent repeats of the behaviour. When over-used, these strategies will cause secondary emotions which make it hard for a child to be open and honest with you about what they are feeling. If a child has to think about how the adult is feeling they will find it hard to focus on finding a solution.

For many people, their own upbringing may have been tough-minded, demanding that emotions were managed quickly and effectively as a sign of self-discipline. While self-discipline is the ultimate long-term aim of behaviour coaching, the route to this goal has to be taken slowly. First the emotional brain needs to be calmed, not suppressed, to allow rational problem solving to take place.

If a child gets the message that strong feelings are unwelcome, they may try to hide them. This is rarely a successful strategy. It will lead the child to swing between the extremes of trying to keep feelings hidden and then swinging back into meltdown when they can no longer manage the swirl of emotions. Often, it can be small things which cause the final meltdown, which leaves the adult both surprised and vaguely irritated. 'What a lot of fuss over nothing.' Emotions are powerful and do not go away satisfactorily unless addressed.

The best way to help a child learn self-discipline is a gradual process of sharing and guiding. Behaviour coaching works at the child's level of understanding to help them resolve any strong feelings which are causing them distress. The process adapts as the child matures and strengthens their ability to make good choices.

## BOX 8   THE FIVE STAGES OF BEHAVIOUR COACHING

### 1. Tune into the child's feelings

This is straightforward if the child's feelings are acted out, as younger children often do, but can be harder when the signs are less direct, like withdrawing or not joining in. You may need to observe what themes come out in a child's imaginary play or their comments about stories, films and TV.

### 2. Make it clear you can resolve this together

Creating closeness and a willingness to share the child's feelings will establish the right environment to teach new skills. Unresolved emotions rarely dissipate and the child's body chemistry is likely to remain in 'flight or fight' mode, so getting in early will also avoid the situation escalating.

### 3. Listen and validate the child's feelings

Aim to enter the child's world so you can reflect back their feelings and help the child accept and understand what they feel. This also allows the child a safe space to step back and see what you see. It breaks the powerful hold that emotion has over the child when all their attention is focused on the object of distress. Encouraging the child to talk helps them to understand themselves, as well as be understood. 'You are feeling angry' is a statement of fact necessary to begin unravelling what is going on.

### 4. Label the feelings

For young children especially, emotions are experienced as unpleasant but indefinable. Children gradually learn to identify what they are feeling through experience and through being given support and the vocabulary to describe what they feel. Children often use words like hate to cover aspects of anger shading from frustration, annoyance and irritability through to dislike and anger. 'I hate you' can mean a variety of things. This can be uncomfortable to hear but by talking together gradually shades of meaning are identified.

Let's listen in on a behaviour coaching session between Tom and his father. Tom is eight years old, and has a younger sister, Lara aged four. She hero-worships her big brother but her following him around is unwelcome. Lara has just come into his room and has started playing with a Lego model he is very proud of. He shouts at her to leave it alone, which she ignores, leading to a scuffle as he tries to push her out of the room.

Here are the steps Tom's father followed to help him decide how to get along better with his sister. Let's assume Dad has let Tom know he understands he is angry and that he wants to help him. They have got to the stage where they are ready to problem solve.

### 5. Problem solving

This is a guided approach which begins by dealing with the immediate situation caused by Tom pushing his sister. The inappropriate behaviour has to be acknowledged before focusing on the future. It is important that Tom understands that his feelings are not the problem, it is his behaviour towards his sister which is unacceptable.

- *Set limits for behaviour:* Dad has to make it clear to Tom that although he understands why he felt frustrated with his sister it was not, and never would be, OK to kick her or hurt her in any way. Dad says: 'I know you are angry but it was not OK to kick your sister,' 'It is never acceptable to hurt people when we are angry with them,' 'We need to find a way for you to work things out with Lara when you disagree.'

- *Identify goals:* Now Dad and Tom will be looking for ways of expressing anger and managing disputes between the siblings. 'How can you get along better with your sister?'

- *Explore options:* If Dad were to give Tom a set of rules it might work but it is likely to crack under pressure. It is better to help Tom come up with a range of options. Dad is aiming for win/win for both children but initially Tom only sees the solution from his own perspective. 'I think she should be banned from coming in my room or playing with my toys.' Dad knows this isn't ideal but decides not to reject this option out of hand. Instead he asks further questions to explore how well it might work in practice. 'When will Lara get to play with you? Is it fair for only you to decide? What else might help you to get on better?' This questioning helps Tom to think of things from his sister's perspective and develop some empathy with her.

- *Weigh up their merits:* They end up with two options: either asking Lara to knock to see if Tom is busy or agreeing that bedrooms are private spaces but offering to play together downstairs or in the garden instead.

- *Making the choice:* Tom decides that he could make it work best if he asked Lara to knock to ask if he was available and if he was busy he could agree a time to come and play a game later. They decide that the next step is to say sorry to Lara and to ask her what she thinks of the plan. Fortunately she is happy with this and can see the advantage of not having her big brother come into her own room either unless she agrees.

It can work to use this approach with both children particularly when it is not clear what happened.

It may not always be possible to use behaviour coaching close to an event. If the child is very unsettled, they might need to be offered some quiet time doing something distracting. 'I realize you are feeling very angry and I do want to help you, but first I think you need some quiet time to help you settle.'

Find something calming and repetitive to help them take their mind off what has happened. Young children are often willing to do a helping task but older children who remain volatile and frequently have outbursts may need a planned strategy of activities which will engage them successfully until they are in a calmer and more receptive state to begin behaviour coaching.

Once the child's rate of breathing and heart rate has settled, you can begin the behaviour coaching cycle acknowledging how they are feeling and working towards a possible solution. You should also look for other signs that the stress response is diminishing like skin being less flushed and of course whether they smile at your jokes.

## 3. Self-motivation

Emotional wellbeing depends upon the ability to make good choices and be motivated to work towards goals which are fulfilling. There is always a conflict between what is available now, which is easy, and working towards something more challenging but worthwhile. Learning to manage distractions and work towards a long-term goal depends on being able to restrain impulsive emotional needs. Motivation is the process whereby we convince ourselves of the greater value of the reward that is some way into the future.

There is a classic experiment from the 1960s exploring the strength of willpower needed for this deferred gratification. Walter Mischel offered four-year-olds in a kindergarten the choice of one marshmallow now or two later if they waited. He then left them alone in the room with the one marshmallow for 15 minutes. These studies have been replicated and filmed showing little ones trying to wait.[28] Some close their eyes, others look away and some seem to be telling themselves things to help them along.

His research is particularly interesting because he followed the children up in high school and found a strong link between the ability to wait at the age of four and achievement scores on SAT tests. This was a better predictor of success than IQ scores. More recently research conducted by Angela Lee Duckworth has identified that extreme persistence or grit is a stronger predictor of high grades at university than IQ or exam results in school.[29]

Planning ahead and goal setting encourages children to see themselves as capable of change and growth. Deferred gratification is essentially an optimistic process that assumes that effort today will pay off tomorrow. Being motivated and having goals raises confidence and self-esteem. Children who learn to set themselves goals both at home and at school are more likely to have positive self-esteem.[30]

## 4. Recognizing emotions in others

Building and sustaining relationships depends on experience and practice. The processes involved in social interaction are very complex. Interestingly, it seems that over the course of evolution we have developed inbuilt systems which help us to learn these skills more easily. Social rules and expectations vary across cultures, so this inner processor seems to help us by working out these rules intuitively so we can fit in. Consequently children are able to pick up social rules which have not been explained to them. Language also has an inner processor, or deep structure, as psychologists call it, which allows a child to infer rules. A child might say 'I runned really fast,' which they have never heard anyone say, because to run is an irregular verb. However, they seem to have worked out that the past tense uses the 'ed' rule. Similarly young children will tell you 'boys don't play with girls' or 'ladies don't drive lorries' depending on what they have noticed happening around them. No one has told them this directly, but it has been inferred from what they see around them.

A basic capacity to recognize other people's feelings is inborn, but needs to be nurtured and developed. Babies become upset when they hear another child cry. Later toddlers will try to comfort another child with a hug or by giving them a toy. Sometimes a child will take their own mother over even when the child's own parent is there. It is clear that a young child's understanding is limited to their own understanding of the world and what they find works for them.

Our social strengths develop when we make full use of our social awareness to respond sensitively and authentically to another person.

*Social awareness* comes from the interplay of these skills:

- *Empathy:* a non-verbal and emotionally based ability to sense what the other person is feeling by picking upon subtle cues such as body language, voice tone and facial expression.

- *Active listening skills:* giving full attention not just to the words but to the pace and emotional tone which will give us a rounded understanding of the other person's communication. We need to focus completely on the other person when they are speaking and stop our attention drifting on to the personal thoughts and feelings sparked by what is said.

- *Theory of mind:* is a cognitive skill which allows us to take another person's perspective and make sense of what they are thinking and feeling. It is a cognitive skill because we need to actively discount what we already know from our own perspective and prevent this from colouring our judgement. This does not start to develop until a child is around four years old.

- *Social knowledge:* is a working knowledge of the social norms and expectations which are relevant to any situation. The demands of any social situation vary on a continuum between formal and more relaxed behaviour. The appropriate behaviour for any situation is based on rules which are rarely actively taught.

## EMPATHY BUILDING

Empathy is an automatic emotional response to another's distress or pain. The family is the original safe space for understanding and sharing the concerns of others. When family members support each other, they help to maintain emotional wellbeing. This creates a virtuous circle of belonging, safety and protection which helps everyone to be in a good place and receive support.

Children find it more difficult to respond with empathy when their own emotions are over-aroused and a threat to their own wellbeing. In children who have not received the support they need to feel protected, empathy may be blunted. They will not have learned to manage their own emotional wellbeing successfully. They remain hyper-aroused and ill at ease with the world. Their attention is focused inward and they have little time or space for the needs of others. An insecure child is more likely to be able to develop their empathy skills with help when this is based on experiences which feel personally safe and detached. This creates some space for the child to step into the other child's shoes without fear or sense of personal threat. Films and stories ensure the child feels safe from the dilemma but able to imagine and explore its impact. Drama can provide a means to play out themes where someone needs help and problems are solved. For younger children small world play and puppets are a useful medium while, for the older child, dance, music and drama can provide safe alternative worlds to explore difficult emotions.

## 5. Developing and maintaining relationships

The need to belong is the most powerful of all motivations, whether it is our bonds within the family, our relationships with friends and partners, or our professional and social contacts. Social skills allow us to 'read' a situation to decide what to do. This needs rapid timing and a fluent and natural response so there are no gaps. Sincerity is also a vital component; when we sense that someone 'is just saying that' for effect we feel manipulated. The skills we depend upon for social success are:

- *Synchrony:* deciding on the correct degree of personal space and how to manage eye contact and body language makes the difference between a pleasant encounter and one which leaves us feeling ill at ease.

- *Rapport:* the ability to connect with someone so they feel recognized and appreciated.

- *Reciprocity/turn taking:* it is important to maintain a healthy balance between speaking and listening to maintain the power balance in the relationship.

- *Openness:* making a connection with someone requires sincerity but varying degrees of self-disclosure depending on the circumstances.

- *Mutual concern:* relationships are built upon a sense of interdependence, where both benefit from the connection. Where the situation is one-sided the relationship may feel unsatisfactory.

Children learn these skills by observation and imitation so good role models linked with opportunities to hone their own social skills are essential. Children observe and internalize knowledge from the adults around them but they also learn from their peers. Children who are slightly more mature and experienced make good role models as the observing child can identify with someone who is not too far out of reach.

For all children managing powerful emotions gives a child confidence and self-belief, which is one side of the emotional wellbeing picture. A deep and satisfying wellbeing needs to move forward from preventing unease into developing the ability to seek out and create positive emotions.

## HOW TO NURTURE POSITIVE EMOTIONS

### A well-rounded life

Emotional wellbeing won't emerge from a charmed life where children are protected from anything that might upset or frustrate them. Like a tender hothouse plant put outside on a winter's day, a child will not be equipped to cope with any drastic change of climate. Children need a set of emotional coping strategies which make it possible to manage whatever happens without being overwhelmed or sidetracked.

Children need to experience the whole range of human emotions to live a full and vibrant life. If we don't experience sadness or disappointment we are unlikely to empathize with others or be motivated to make changes to unsatisfactory circumstances. To do this we have to learn how to tune in to our own and other people's feelings and use this knowledge to manage our actions. In a safe environment, a child's main exposure to fear and anger will be through story and drama, rather than real life. Stories are so much more than entertainment, they are a chance for children to glimpse other worlds and learn in safety and comfort.

Emotional wellbeing is not merely a set of personal skills to boost self-esteem but is also the foundation for fulfilling relationships. Emotional wellbeing has a profound impact on all aspects of children's development: their personal wellbeing, their social skills and their ability to focus and learn. Children who are emotionally vulnerable are not only at the mercy of a kaleidoscope of changing emotions but are also less likely to learn or make satisfactory friendships.

## Flourishing can be learned: boosting positive emotions

It is no surprise that the evidence points to a strong connection between emotional wellbeing, good health, satisfying relationships and success at school or at work. You might assume that wellbeing is the result of being healthy and successful but evidence suggests that this connection is flipped the other way round. Several studies which have followed people over a long period found that generally happy people fared better on various measures including living a longer, healthier life, having a successful marriage and achieving career goals. Other research has estimated that while temperament and circumstances do play a role in happiness, around 40 per cent can be altered by what you think and do.[31] This is more than enough to make a significant difference. Children can be shown how to get on the right track to boost their positive emotions and ensure that they flourish.

## The emotional brain and wellbeing

While our physical environment and lifestyle has changed enormously over the centuries, the basic workings of our emotional brain have not. As we discovered when exploring emotional competence, the emotions which serve to warn us about potential threats far outnumber the emotions which create happiness. This can lead to a constant low-grade sense that all is not well, even when there is no objective cause.

## Counteracting the negativity bias

Unfortunately, our emotions do not lie dormant until something big comes along; they seem to be permanently switched on ready for action. They monitor the world around us day and night, setting off their alarms when something may be amiss. This can be as simple as the apprehension we feel when entering a new situation, or the irritability of waiting for the postman to arrive with an important letter. Left to their own devices emotions do not take well to uncertainty or change. Our protective emotions can easily become overactive on our behalf, unless we learn how to downgrade their red alerts, and upgrade the time we spend creating positive thoughts and experiences.

## The impact of the stress response

If we leave our emotions to tick along on their own, with no active help from us, the result is far from good. Below the surface, too, emotions have a direct impact on our physical health, as it is their role to orchestrate the chemical and physical reactions needed to take action. The feelings we gain from an emotional reaction are only the tip of the iceberg, below the surface a huge emergency response drill is being organized, affecting the whole body.

The protective emotions all switch on the 'flight, fight or freeze' response, otherwise known as the stress response. When we are angry or fearful, our body starts to prepare for action. Disgust and surprise create a startle reaction which jolts us to stop what we are doing and reconsider our actions. Sadness and shame both create a slowing down which protects us from continuing in a direction which might lead to further harm.

All these physical reactions are powerful and take us over, so that there is no chance of business as usual. Even at a lower level, of irritation rather than anger, anxiety rather than fear, we still become distracted and are unlikely to be fully alert and focused.

## The calming effect of positive emotions

In contrast, the emotions that are linked to love and enjoyment have a powerful effect on wellbeing. They calm and soothe us while also deepening our connection with others and increasing our sense of security. Below the surface an equal but opposite process takes place with 'feel good hormones' ensuring the heart rate is settled and that the blood flow returns to the digestion, and to make learning and memory possible again. All these processes are shut down under the stress response.

Now that we all have such busy and stressful lives, time for enjoyment can get crowded out by the perpetual demands of daily life. Enjoyment may have become a spare time activity, rather than the central theme of how we live our lives. Enjoyment is not a bonus; it is what nature requires to work her magic. We owe it to children to create enjoyment in their lives because it is the oxygen of wellbeing which creates the physical and psychological states necessary to flourish. Just as exercise is essential for physical health, enjoyment and love are vital to emotional wellbeing.

## Positivity research

Barbara Fredrickson, Professor at the University of Carolina, Chapel Hill has led research into what brings balance and wellbeing into busy lives.[32] She has established that the positive emotions 'undo' the effect of the hard-driving, negative emotions which mobilize the potentially harmful stress response. Our ancestors needed short bursts of energy to protect themselves and then things quickly returned to normal. In contrast, now, low-level but insistent demands can keep the stress response permanently revved up.

The positive emotions are vital because they turn off the stress response and replace the potentially toxic chemical cocktail of stress hormones for a different recipe which calms us physically while focusing and sustaining our attention. Fredrickson calls this the 'broaden and build' effect. The 'broaden and build' effect is first seen in babies' interactions with their mothers, allowing happy babies to bond and learn about their world through play. Happy babies are alert and interested in what is going on around them. They are relaxed and ready to learn. The more often they are helped to be alert and positive the more interest they can take in the world around them. In contrast, distress will claim their total attention, turning their focus inwards and will shut out the world.

Throughout childhood, young people depend on adult support to help them experience fun and success. Children are easily unsettled, as their finely tuned emotional awareness is designed to be on the lookout for threats. Adults, who accept this demanding role, can offer running repairs to help children sort out their fears and disappointments. They accept that distress overwhelms children at a faster and more frequent rate than is typical of adults and so children need a different lifestyle and support.

Earlier we identified the 'negativity bias' which is nature's emotional default position. Barbara Fredrickson and her colleagues have identified that we need at least a 3:1 ratio of positive to negative emotional experiences for wellbeing. That is unlikely to happen by chance. Everyone needs to develop strategies to over-ride the freewheeling emotional brain.

## Raw emotion and impulsive behaviour

The messages we receive from our emotional brain are exaggerated and insistent. It is their role to protect but they often catastrophize. After all, they are there to keep us alive; they could not do that successfully by being low key and saying 'Sorry to bother you but you might want to notice X if you have the time.' Our emotional brain *shouts loudly* and has no volume control.

Children, in particular, are novices when it comes to listening to their emotional signals. An unkind word from a friend becomes the end of the friendship; a bump in a busy playground becomes an assault rather than an accident. Children definitely need support to stop and question whether what they are feeling is true. We will examine in detail how children can be helped to develop an optimistic frame of reference when we explore resilience.

Children who react impulsively are likely also to behave aggressively and in an antisocial way. The emotional brain's protective effect does not weigh up consequences or think of the needs of others. We see that in the daily catalogue of playground woes, 'who did what to whom' has to regularly be unravelled by patient staff. We would be horrified if a workplace coffee break descended into similar chaos but we have come to accept that this is just what kids do. That may be so, but children can dread playtimes if they feel unable to stay safe and happy. So what can we do to raise the bar, giving children a generally higher dose of the feel good emotions to reduce the ease with which the stress response kicks in?

## Building emotional wellbeing: over-riding the emotional brain

Positive emotions *undo* the effect of stress and *broaden and build* the focus of attention. The more positive experiences a child has, the more that creates the inner calm which bolsters learning and protects against stress. Given that children have an amplified negativity bias they definitely need a little help. To help children reduce impulsive behaviour you need both a short-term and a long-term plan. Here are some suggestions.

### BOX 9   TEN WAYS TO NURTURE POSITIVE EMOTIONS ON A DAY TO DAY BASIS

1. Make time for children to get involved in self-discovery play which uses their strengths and helps develop a positive self-image. The feel good factor can last beyond the time spent in play and also creates the mindset that says I am capable. I know I have said this before but it really is the number one strategy for psychological wellbeing.

2. Be realistic about how much time a child can happily occupy themselves for. Trouble starts when children get frustrated. A light touch monitoring avoids things escalating. Don't expect children to just play unless you know they have a well-developed imagination.

3. Be ready to step in with ideas and materials which keep the play going. Suggest what else they can do or surprise them with an unusual idea or plaything that isn't generally available to get things back on track.

4. Children spend a lot of time struggling with things they can't yet do, so create celebrations and special moments regularly to acknowledge effort and draw their attention to their achievements.

5. Encourage children to use their strengths by offering positive and specific praise which shows you have recognized that this is something important and personal for them.

6. Notice what energizes children and makes them smile or laugh. Help them find more time for what gives genuine enjoyment.

7. Look out for the excitement that rapidly flips over into aggression. This is adrenaline fuelled and stress related. The use of computer games and gadgets seems more likely to lead to this kind of hyper-excitement which ends in tears.

8. Ensure there is also time for light-hearted fun with others. Non-competitive games work well especially if there is an element of chance to help younger children not feel outclassed.

9. Many children don't do sitting down very well. They are expected to do a lot of it: car journeys, lessons at school and home entertainments such as TV need counterbalancing with something more energetic.

10. Active outdoor and rough and tumble play gives children a natural high from energetic activity. Also, time outdoors, particularly in open green space, has a calming effect even after a short leisurely walk.

## The four pillars of positive emotions

Positive emotions help us to grow and make constructive changes in our lives. Barbara Fredrickson's concept of 'broaden and build' expands our horizons and creates the zest and energy to take on time-consuming and long-term plans. Positive emotions work even better when they offer high-quality relationships with others.

Optimism, hope, gratitude and forgiveness are not strictly emotions; Martin Seligman describes them as character strengths, but they are useful to mention here as they play a complementary role in building emotional wellbeing.

Children who tend to be very focused on the present can find it difficult to see beyond what is happening right now. The four pillars of positive emotions (Figure 2) show children how to lift their head high and look to the far horizon.

| Optimism | Hope |
|---|---|
| 'the tendency to expect the best in all things' | 'a desire for something and confidence in the possibility of fulfilment' |
| The benefits of optimism are: | The benefits of hope are: |
| • acknowledging that things can change for the better<br>• an ability to manage setbacks as temporary<br>• gaining the energy and determination to sustain effort<br>• a focus on a desired and uplifting goal. | • confidence in the future<br>• a creative approach to restart stalled projects<br>• an ability to live with discomfort in the short term<br>• an active focus on a goal<br>• a positive 'can do' attitude. |
| **Gratitude** | **Forgiveness** |
| 'a feeling of thankfulness for gifts or favours' | 'to cease to blame someone or to grant pardon for a mistake' |
| The benefits of gratitude are: | The benefits of forgiveness are: |
| • a deepening of bonds with others<br>• the security of feeling valued and supported<br>• an awareness of the importance of relationships<br>• a fostering of mutual dependency. | • repairing the bond with someone close<br>• avoiding the negative spiral of resentment and anger<br>• regaining the 'broaden and build' effect of positive emotions. |

Figure 2: The four pillars of positive emotions

## Increasing the positivity ratio

Children can be encouraged to do more that they will enjoy but in reality children have limited control over their lives and will need adults to at least enable them to boost their positive experiences. Another aspect of positivity is ensuring that children capture and hold on to positive feelings to prolong them and extend the impact.

## Practical activities to boost positivity

Sometimes life is routine and does not offer opportunities for enjoyment, then we have to draw on the past or anticipate the future to shift our mood from dissatisfied to content. Children tend to live in the moment, so good times may rush by without the full depth of appreciation that would have more lasting impact. Here are five techniques to boost a child's focus on the positive to help them capture and prolong positive experiences.

When you encourage children to fully concentrate on their present experience, it deepens awareness and increases the chances that those experiences will be remembered. When you don't pay attention to something, it is much less likely to be recalled later. Below are some practical ways to encourage that focus of attention in a pleasurable way.

## SAVOURING

Savouring is giving something your full, undivided attention so that you can appreciate every tiny detail. You can introduce children to savouring something by eating something delicate and delicious together. This is an activity which is always well received. You will need to encourage children to do every step slowly while fully focusing on what they do. Take a small piece of a favourite food and take your time to notice everything about it. Look at the shape, the colour, notice the aroma. Before you pop it in your mouth are you salivating in anticipation? Then slowly eat it, taking as long as you can. Talk about the experience afterwards to share other dimensions of what was noticed.

## SCRAPBOOKS AND DIARIES

Children enjoy keeping a record of special outings or occasions. Photographs can be effective but if taken by adults they lack the engagement which this activity needs. Consider drawing, writing and collage as ways to get younger children fully immersed in the experience. Older children may prefer to keep a personal diary.

## TREASURE BOXES

Children enjoy collecting mementoes of a day out which can be kept in a special box and returned to at other times to relive the experience. Children between the ages of four and nine are often avid collectors. You may need to actively help younger children explore why something is special enough to keep and what it will remind them of. Not all treasures will be of lasting significance and children can choose which ones to keep and why, when they make room for a new collection.

## CREATIVE VISUALIZATION

This is a useful skill which older children can build on because it doesn't need any physical props. It can be done anywhere and at any time that suits. It's a bit like day dreaming, but more constructive, and less wistful. You may need to talk children through, step by step, in the early days but later they can do this independently.

As the image builds in the mind, the relaxation effect of the positive emotions begins to flow. Children may need some help at first, to decide what and where they are visiting in their mind's eye. Make sure it is somewhere where they are relaxed and happy and that they can picture the scene in detail. Some children take to this very easily, especially if they are able to visualize an image clearly. Other children may need to practice but will get there if they persevere. Making general statements can help children into the process.

Here is a possible script:

> *Imagine yourself in a place that makes you happy. What can you see around you? How clear are the colours? What are you feeling as you look around you? Do you feel happy, relaxed and smiling? What can you hear in this lovely place, are there voices, music or perhaps birds are singing? Are there any pleasant aromas like flowers or delicious food? Sit quietly enjoying this lovely place and feel your body becoming more and more relaxed.*

Leave some time in silence for further enjoyment. You can tell if someone is struggling to engage with the experience by their body language and facial expression. This will also provide cues as to when to bring them back into the room. Using the same relaxed and gentle voice say 'It will soon be time to leave this lovely place but remember you can go back there by yourself. I will count down from five and I want you then to open your eyes feeling alert, happy and relaxed.' This technique is often used in relaxation classes but it should be a staple technique for all children to learn to lift their mood when necessary.

### IMAGINATIVE REHEARSAL

This allied technique allows a positive practice run on something you are working towards. The benefits lie in the anticipation of the final experience, which is emotionally uplifting, and the practical advantage of going over exactly what you have to do to get there. This approach is used by athletes to visualize their best performance and to imaginatively enter an event which they are currently training for. Young people can use this to imagine an exam going well and to check with themselves what they might do to ensure they perform at their best. Children who are not yet fluent readers can imagine themselves reading a challenging book to a delighted audience or writing a letter to a family member fluently and with no hesitation.

## Group activities to boost positivity

There are so many ways to encourage children to have fun together: games, dancing, music and drama are all long-established life enhancers. You can do things together at home and seek out local classes which might interest your child. In a school setting, time has to be scheduled in the timetable and activities planned. There has been a tendency to crowd out 'the arts' as an optional extra but while these activities are all delightful for their own sake they also serve a vital role to create the positive balance of emotions that help children to learn.

## SUMMARY

- Emotional learning is essential to guide our decision making.
- Emotional learning lays down memories which can make children feel secure or leave them vulnerable.
- Vulnerable children can be helped to modify their view of the world when new and trusting relationships build an alternate vision.
- The eight primary families of emotions are there to protect us. There are six that identify threat and only two which build security and enjoyment.
- The 'negativity bias' needs careful management to avoid stress and mental health difficulties.
- Emotional competence will help children identify and manage their own emotions and recognize the needs of others.
- A positivity ratio of at least 3:1 is vital for emotional wellbeing.
- Activities for both individuals and groups which build positive emotions are needed on a daily basis so that young people learn how to create their own positivity.

Factor 3

# Positive Communication
## Building Trust and Fulfilling Relationships

### Overview

In this chapter we will explore what can raise the quality of the communication you have with a child from mundane to magical. As you develop your conscious competence in positive communication, you can help form positive and satisfying relationships.

There are three core elements of positive communication which are essential to building good relationships:

1. the eight positive communication principles, which boost rapport and trust

2. appreciative attention, which aims to boost confidence through positive praise and feedback

3. encouraging communication, in particular an approach called active and constructive responding, which ensures a sincere and appreciative response.

## BUILDING POSITIVE COMMUNICATION

In the previous chapter we explored how the emotional brain has a 'protect and detect' role for the young child. The cortex, or thinking part of the brain, matures slowly as the child learns new skills and brain connections are formed. The brain continues to develop and connect until adulthood.

Children slowly develop the skill to manage their emotions and learn how to balance the pressing demands of the emotional brain with a more reasoned approach based on the workings of the cortex. Throughout childhood and adolescence, the battle to integrate the two minds continues, making adult support invaluable to help young people make decisions which allow them to flourish. We will see how the eight principles of positive communication offer a child effective support and influence.

## How positive communication supports the growing child

Positive communication is the glue which holds relationships together. We are hardwired to tune into others via mirror neurons which cause us to reflect back the actions and expressions we see. This creates a synchrony between people which is automatic. If you smile at someone as you pass by, often they will smile back, then the look in their eyes which follows shows that they have just registered the action. 'Why did I do that? Who was she? Do I know her?'

The amazing capacity to copy what we see so accurately is down to these specialist cells in the brain. Have you ever wondered how people manage to learn dance moves with minimum effort? They pick up information about what someone else is doing and help us to tune in very closely and accurately. Mirror neurons are also partly protective, in that they alert us to what someone is doing when we are not paying direct attention, so that we become aware of anything in our immediate environment which could be threatening. However, their function is primarily positive in helping people to connect fluently with minimal effort.

Mirror neurons alert our attention to the other person's actions. Have you noticed the urge to imitate what another person is doing is sometimes so powerful that you can't help copying? At other times we may not be aware of someone's actions but copy them involuntarily.

Next time you are having coffee with a friend, notice whether your postures are similar and if you reach for your drink at the same time. Having positive feelings towards someone increases the likelihood of this mirroring and matching effect.

## Our need to connect

This willingness to connect with others is hardwired, what Daniel Goleman in his book *Social Intelligence*[33] calls 'neural wifi'. This natural sociability has been essential to human evolution; it serves both a child's need for protection and also helps adults form communities which are stronger and more likely to survive hardships such as famine and attack. In our more individualistic twenty-first-century western culture, that reliance on others to survive has been replaced by money. What you need but can't produce yourself is bought, the need for a relationship between producer and consumer is broken. However, our innate need to connect remains intact and central to our wellbeing even when it isn't expressed. People who become socially isolated are more likely to feel anxious and depressed. They feel vulnerable.

### Developing positive communication

The role of positive communication has a triple effect:

1. It gives children the skills which make relationships satisfying.
2. It builds strong relationships with an adult who can support and protect.
3. It creates the security which makes children feel confident and able to play and learn.

### What close relationships contribute to wellbeing

When we have a bond with someone, it does far more than lift our mood. We experience positive emotions which broaden and build our energy level and increase our interest in the world around us. The cascade of feel good hormones surges through our system. These chemicals have a huge impact, first they make us feel good, and then they bond us to the person who made us feel that way. We are more likely to want to be with that person again because we enjoy their company. At another level these feel good hormones are also the body's messenger systems which coordinate growth and repair in the body and brain. Being in a good place with others is actually physically good for us too. While it is important for adults, it is absolutely essential for a child's healthy, happy development.

### The beginnings of positive communication

Positive communication starts at a sensory and emotional level from birth, it is largely non-verbal although the voice is also important.

Body language, facial expression, and tone of voice are the powerful building blocks of rapport from the beginning. They are also the initial impression makers which we intuitively react to whenever we meet new people. Usually they operate below the radar, something we do not think about. Rapport skills are largely intuitive and spontaneous. We signal our fondness or wariness of someone without even thinking about it. It can also be difficult to mask our feelings when we are being polite.

If we are to understand how to support children to feel secure and confident we need to be conscious of these essential building blocks of non-verbal, positive communication which make relationships work successfully.

- How do children know that they can count upon your protection and support?

- What shows them that you care about them and want them to do well?

- Do they feel secure about asking you to do something for them when they are challenged, frustrated or confused?

There are eight elements of positive communication which build satisfying relationships. They are taken from in-depth studies of parent/child relationships which are flourishing.[34]

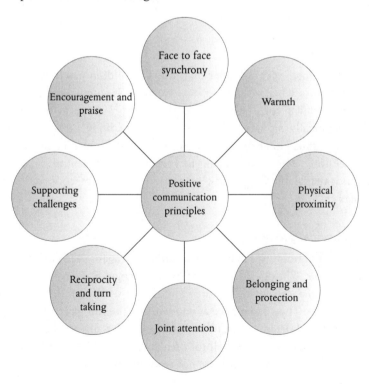

Figure 3: The eight positive communication principles

When we become consciously aware of how these elements work then we can actively look for ways of making our communication with children more effective. Perhaps you could pair up with someone you trust and take turns to offer feedback. If you work in a setting which offers co-coaching or the use of video this can be really helpful. Start by sharing what goes well; finding your strengths means you can actively build on them in situations where you may otherwise not have done so.

---

## BOX 10   THE EIGHT POSITIVE COMMUNICATION PRINCIPLES

### 1. Face to face synchrony

A strong relationship builds from plenty of mutual eye contact, smiling and, better still, laughter. From an early age babies study faces, both real ones and pictures, and show a strong interest in communication. The eye contact is mutual and not forced. In contrast, looking for a prolonged time at someone who is averting their gaze has the opposite effect and can be hostile. Synchrony has to be mutual and is part of a wider pattern of turn taking.

### 2. Warmth

Tone of voice speaks louder than words. Children may not always pay attention to what we say, but how we say it is automatically registered. Is the adult's voice soothing or threatening? A warm tone of voice automatically signals safety and allows the body's alarm systems to relax. Adults under pressure often signal their stressed feelings through voice tone, even when trying to keep the words neutral. Warmth is a fundamental building block of rapport and makes cooperation more likely.

### 3. Physical proximity

Touch and holding can be very soothing but again needs to be mutually acceptable. Sitting side by side is less demanding than face to face contact and can make it more comfortable when a child is getting to know you. They can glance at you without the full glare of making eye contact, and decide when to look away, which manages the building up of eye contact. It can be helpful with younger children to physically get down to their level so you are not towering over them.

### 4. Belonging and protection

Children feel safe when their environment is familiar and when they are with someone they know. In large groups children can feel unsettled, unless the group has a strong sense of identity. In a newly formed group it repays the time spent to ensure all children know they are accepted and belong. The need to feel safe and to seek adult protection is obvious in young children but the older, insecure child can also be unsettled by uncertainty. Children are primed to react to strange people or situations as part of their primitive survival strategy. A sense of belonging switches off that stress response and allows children to relax and take an interest in what is happening around them.

### 5. Joint attention

Rapport and warmth allows the adult and child to share their experience. A mother will draw the child's attention to something that might be of interest and later the child wants to share things that interest them. This sharing is the beginning of learning and nurtures both curiosity and a trust in the adult's ability to make life interesting. Joint attention is a two-way process and adults often need to build that personal connection before formal teaching is successful. Children who have not had a rich experience of shared communication in early life may need to become used to working together.

### 6. Reciprocity and turn taking

When an adult is in harmony with a child there is an almost 'dance like' pattern of imitating and turn taking which can be small movements or glances but which serve to deepen the relationship. It is not unlike the private jokes of new partners who are constantly referencing each other. The adult takes their pace from the child, neither too fast or too slow, to mirror back excitement energetically or take a slow more relaxed pace to soothe and reassure.

### 7. Supporting challenges

Young children have much to learn and this can be frustrating. A secure child will have had encouragement to try new things in a carefully managed way. How can you avoid taking the child too far outside their comfort zone?

### 8. Encouragement and praise

The attentive adult is familiar with what a child can do and encourages them to strengthen their skills. Encouragement works best when a child knows that you understand them and will give them step by step support.

The positive communication principles are important because they:

- make relationships work better
- encourage language growth and development
- boost the physical biochemistry which calms a child
- reduce stress and frustration.

In summary, they create what Barbara Fredrickson calls the 'broaden and build' effect, as we discovered in the previous chapter (also see the worksheet on p.109).

## Positive communication stimulates the brain

The relationship between parent and child has an almost miraculous effect in kick starting all areas of development. How this works is directly connected to the hormonal messenger systems which stimulate growth and development. The baby's brain depends on love to begin to grow and develop. Behind this seemingly romantic statement is a body of neuroscientific research which has examined how learning takes place.[35]

A baby's brain at birth has more brain cells than will ever be required, but there are actually very few working connections at first. This flexibility allows adaptive learning so children can learn any skills they need in their community. This is in complete contrast to animal brains which have substantial pre-set instinctual patterns of behaviour which are quickly turned on by early experience.

For the young child this openness to learning has both advantages and costs. The baby's brain is unfinished, and the child is vulnerable and totally dependent. Learning takes place slowly and the child continues to require attentive and protective care. Human learning doesn't unfold like a flower grows from a seed; it is not there in embryonic form. It can only happen when high-quality care provides a safe base for the child to explore the world and learn.

Equally, a child who is neglected and lacks social stimulation risks seriously impaired development. This was confirmed by examining the progress of children brought up with gross neglect in orphanages in Romania. One of the poignant misconceptions about institutional care was that physical care alone was thought to be enough. The history of orphanages demonstrates that food and shelter without loving care is little short of disastrous. Children survive but are grossly developmentally delayed and without stimulation and education remain this way and can become severely mentally disabled. Fortunately, children can go on to make good progress if they are given intensive support post-adoption, although recovery is slow and difficult.

## The child's developing brain and capacity for learning

Cognitive neuroscience research in the past decade has substantially increased our understanding of how the human brain develops. We will visit some of the basics so that we understand why positive relationships and communication on the outside are so crucial to what happens on the inside. Love directly shapes the child's developing brain.

As the child learns, brain cells connect, making nerve pathways which can strengthen a learned response each time it is repeated. Neuroscientists, who are the experts in this area, talk about brain architecture as the forming and shaping of different areas which take place as a result of learning. As some learning pathways are formed, other cells are 'pruned' in the surrounding area. While we may think that having lots of brain cells is a good thing in itself, it seems that what is most important is for the strong pathways of nerve cells link together to work efficiently. The brain in adult life still has considerable spare capacity. You could compare the mass of brain cells a baby has to seedlings sown too thickly in a seed tray, unless some are thinned out none of them will do well.

This sculpting of the brain depends on learning and experience. As new skills are learned, and new experiences remembered, the connections are made between brain cells. The more frequently something happens, the stronger the nerve pathways between cells become.

The feel good hormones which create the experience of love, contentment, relaxation or elation all allow the body to be in full growth and repair mode. The release of the hormone oxytocin and the neurotransmitter dopamine creates a feeling of wellbeing for both adult and child. In addition the connection between adult and child provides many opportunities to do things together when a child is calm and receptive to learning. Learning takes place in the presence of these benign hormones, not only because of the social connection triggered, but also because on the inside these neurotransmitters are the building blocks which coordinate the physical development of nerve pathways.

The reverse situation occurs with cortisol and adrenaline overload: we become preoccupied with our emotional unease and can't concentrate. The 'flight or fight' messengers shut down the growth and repair processes to allow for only key functions necessary for this state of emergency. This conserves energy for doing battle or running away. We breathe faster and our heart pumps more blood to muscles. Increased adrenaline will make sure we feel less pain if injured, and our blood will clot more quickly to reduce blood loss. This is an amazing process which protects us and helps us survive but it is completely opposed to learning. Blood to the cortex, the thinking area of the brain, is reduced and thinking and memory are effectively shut off. Naturally you don't want to be thinking about what's happening if your life is at stake do you?

Fortunately for us, stress in the twenty-first century is rarely a life and death matter, but unfortunately for the child, this full-blown emergency process happens every time, even when they are just a little spooked. When a child's emotional fire alarm goes off too often, or stays on for too long, a child will not be able to learn effectively under stress. In short, healthy brain development depends on low levels of stress. Low levels of stress come from being supported via positive communication to keep the emotional brain under control.

We know that a child's growth and development depends on these 'happy hormones' to allow focused concentration and engagement in work or play. They are as necessary to learning as nutritious food is essential to the body. Every adult needs to be confident of how to create a positive environment to switch on the 'happy hormones' for a child and to disengage the emotional brain from going into survival mode.

## Using and strengthening positive communication

Encouraging children to be relaxed and confident communicators depends on both their direct experience and what they observe. Box 11 lists ten strategies which increase rapport.

### BOX 11   TEN WAYS TO BUILD POSITIVE COMMUNICATION WITH A CHILD

1. Position yourself at eye level with the child so you can read each other's expressions without being too full on.
2. Angle yourself towards the child to build a connection without being too in their face.

3. Notice how the child responds to your presence, are they reassured or wary? Adjust your reactions accordingly.

4. Make use of smiling and humour.

5. Match your responses to the child's; what you do should mirror the child's behaviour. This should be a low-key reflecting back of their body language rather than a full on direct imitation which is unsettling for anyone.

6. Nodding and encouraging expressions support the child without the need for words.

7. Pay attention to what the child is focused on; let them know you are sharing their interest by body language and expression.

8. Warmth is communicated clearly through tone of voice, and sounds like ah, umm, oh can signal your appreciation if you don't want to distract the child from their task.

9. Sometimes just being there is enough, and working alongside rather than face to face supports the child's independence.

10. Be willing to help but don't jump in, let the child tell you what would be helpful by a word or a glance.

### BOX 12   TEN WAYS TO BUILD NON-VERBAL POSITIVE COMMUNICATION WITH CHILDREN IN A GROUP

1. Consider starting the session with one of the positivity boosters such as savouring or creative visualization.

2. When you are in the company of several children address them individually as often as possible. When you focus on any child give them your full, undivided attention even if it lasts only as long as a smile.

3. Trust in your ability to rapidly sense how things are within the group and scan the room regularly to pick up signals of anyone who may need your support.

4. Children also pick up signs quickly and a gesture or facial expression can reassure them from across the room.

5. Keep moving and drop in on children briefly to keep that connection as well as to offer practical help.

6. Encourage children to become fully absorbed by making materials available while offering low-key support.

7.  Use voice tone to encourage without interrupting the flow of what is happening.

8.  Boost positivity in the room via smiling, laughter and fun activities appropriate to the age group.

9.  Reinforce what is going well so that children know you have recognized their efforts.

10. Recognize children's need for independence by being available to help but not diving in to correct or make suggestions too often.

## EXPLORING AND BOOSTING YOUR OWN POSITIVE COMMUNICATION

### When are you at your best?

We all have situations which bring out the best in us. Reflecting on what works for you is the best place to start. Your personal communication strengths may be something you have given little thought to so far. Increasing your awareness over the coming weeks will help you identify what works for you and how you can make best use of your strengths in communication. You may choose to make a daily note of three things that went well. This is a variation of the three good things exercise which is known to make us happier.[36]

### Observe people you admire

Everyone has their own style, and you will know people who you think have great rapport with their child or with the children they know through work. You can use the positive communication principles (see the downloadable form on the following page) to see how these principles influence this person's rapport with children. (I'm not suggesting you slavishly copy someone else, more that you adapt something here and there from all the fantastic people you know.)

### Learning together

If you have a willing friend or work colleague you can explore the contact principles practically using these exercises. Positive communication is powerful when experienced first hand. Find a place where you can be uninterrupted and enjoy role playing at full tilt. You will see exactly what works when you act out your role, don't be too shy or polite.

## Positive communication principles

|  | Adult observations | Child's response |
|---|---|---|
| 1. Face to face synchrony |  |  |
| 2. Warmth |  |  |
| 3. Physical proximity |  |  |
| 4. Belonging and protection |  |  |
| 5. Joint attention |  |  |
| 6. Reciprocity and turn taking |  |  |
| 7. Supporting challenges |  |  |
| 8. Encouragement and praise |  |  |

✓

# ACTIVITY 1: EXPLORING THE IMPACT OF POSITIVE NON-VERBAL COMMUNICATION

Take turns to tell each other about a hobby or interest which you love. You want to choose something you can talk about naturally without having to think too hard so you can observe how your partner is reacting.

**Person A:** Your role is to talk about a hobby; your partner is listening rather than joining in the conversation. Allow two minutes which is enough time to see what effect your partner has on your conversational flow.

**Person B:** Your role is to listen and to focus on encouraging your partner via eye contact, smiling, leaning forward, nods and anything else you know will show you are interested even though you can't join the conversation.

Now swap roles and repeat.

## Points for discussion

- How did it feel to talk knowing you had your partner's full attention?
- Discuss what helped you to feel relaxed and confident as you were talking.
- What did your partner do that was especially encouraging?
- What did you notice that let you know that your partner was listening?

# ACTIVITY 2: EXPLORING THE IMPACT OF NEGATIVE NON-VERBAL COMMUNICATION

Choose another topic of conversation if necessary, although if you have plenty left to say do carry on.

**Person A:** Talk about your hobby for two minutes as before.

**Person B:** This time it is your role is to do anything and everything you can to show you are not interested. Look away, lean back in your chair, yawn and say uh huh in a dull voice…anything that will give a non-verbal message that you are disengaged.

Now swap roles and repeat. You may need a minute or two to get back in rapport before you discuss the impact of the exercise.

## Points for discussion

- How did it feel to talk knowing that your partner was not paying attention?
- Discuss how you felt as this progressed. What were the physical and emotional effects?
- How well could you maintain the flow of what you were saying?
- What did your partner do that was especially discouraging?
- What were the more blatant actions which signalled that your partner was not listening?
- What were the subtle actions which signalled that your partner was not listening?

## NEXT STEPS: BUILDING RAPPORT

After you've done the activities, discuss what will help you build rapport easily with children.

- How easy was it to talk when you were in rapport?
- What did you notice that made a special impact?
- What can you take from this to help you at times when giving a child your full attention isn't easy? We often find this difficult when we are busy with something else or when the thoughts in our head are demanding our attention.
- Note three things you can do to build rapport in situations you find difficult.
- Why not tell your role play partner what you plan to do and agree to compare how things have gone at a later date.

## APPRECIATIVE ATTENTION AND POSITIVE FEEDBACK

### Encouraging children to be confident communicators

The number of times a child makes contact is closely linked to how receptive the adult is.[37] When children are quickly responded to they will continue to be keen to communicate. They will also develop a larger vocabulary than those children who adults miss opportunities to talk and listen to. While early experience is undoubtedly important, it continues to be vital to maximize language skills throughout our lives.

Children quickly identify friendly adults who they feel comfortable with and recognize the positive communication principles intuitively. So when you are confidently using them you will find your relationship becomes more natural, relaxed and sincere. Children will be more drawn to you because they have rapport with you quickly and easily.

How can you develop communication further, encouraging a child to talk to you in a relaxed and friendly way? Children respond well to an approach called appreciative attention, which encourages them to talk about what is important to them.

### Developing speaking and listening skills

Rapport is the primary building block of communication that helps you connect and feel comfortable together. Once a connection is established then language supplies the powerful tools to find out more. Children need good language skills to bolster wellbeing; with poorly developed language, children struggle to share both their triumphs and their challenges.

## The power of language

Language is a skill unique to humans, which enables us to do a number of amazing things. Language:

- lets us share our thoughts and be understood

- builds relationships and deepens intimacy

- helps us to think and reason

- allows us make sense of our experience

- unifies our experience: something we see, hear, touch and taste is given a name and the various dimensions become linked

- helps us to hold on to knowledge via detailed memory

- works to develop our sense of who we are. Language intensifies conscious awareness; being able to observe and capture our experience through this sense of self creates our unique personal identity.

For all these reasons, helping children to use language effectively is pivotal to personal, social development and wellbeing. Making time and space for children to talk about their interests is vital, it encourages children to notice and capture their experience. As children share an experience they become more aware of both what happened and why it was important.

## Appreciative attention

Gaining and keeping a child's attention is more likely when a child is comfortable and not preoccupied with the demands of the emotional brain. Positive communication starts with good rapport which shows that you are able and willing to help. As children become more proficient with language this becomes the medium for sharing. Appreciative attention has a formative role in the early years and continues to have an impact across adolescence. As children become more capable of two-way conversation active constructive responding becomes equally important, as we shall see later.

## Helping children to communicate

Language is a building block of both thinking and learning. The more experience a child has of using language effectively, the better their skills and the greater the likelihood of educational success.

Language skills depend upon three elements:

1. attention and listening skills

2. spoken language

3. understanding what is said to you.

These skills develop from birth and continue to make rapid progress over the pre-school years. Vocabulary and the use of more advanced grammar continue to grow across childhood. However, by the age of six or seven children have mastered significant skills which allow them to communicate effectively and listen attentively enough to sustain formal teaching and learning. Attention and listening skills in particular continue to mature between the ages of four and seven, making it increasingly possible for children to switch their attention between what they are doing and what the adult is saying.

## Give me a child until they are seven

Children who are ready for formal education need to be capable of sustained and attentive listening. To be ready and able to listen a child needs to have been heard and understood.

Appreciative attention encourages the child to talk and the adult to listen. It gives children a chance to share their enthusiasms without too much adult direction. It is not unusual for adults to unbalance a conversation with lots of helpful advice which breaks the child's train of thought and redirects the course of the conversation.

Appreciative attention encourages the adult to support the child's learning by giving praise and encouragement. At a practical level you help to stage manage situations behind the scenes so the child can play and learn at a level which is likely to lead to progress and success.

## Moving a child's comfort zone a little further forward

Children respond to an encouraging adult who offers lots of praise and specific feedback. It boosts their confidence and will inspire them to try something new. The importance of a close relationship was recognized by the psychologist Lev Vygotsky who referred to this as scaffolding the child's learning.[38]

## How to use appreciative attention

The purpose of appreciative attention is to encourage a child to talk and become more aware of what they are doing. Appreciative attention helps to focus the child's attention and increase their awareness. For young children this stimulates language growth, while for the older child it encourages thinking and reflection. To encourage a child to talk you may need to facilitate the conversation.

- *Offer an enthusiastic but neutral comment to open the conversation:* 'You have been working at that … for a while now.' Pause and leave space for thinking and a reply. If children are really absorbed in their task they may not welcome an interruption so if you sense this you may need to keep it light. Acknowledge what the child is doing, 'I think you are enjoying this.'

- *Offer some positive feedback:* noticing comments are a valuable strategy which is appreciated by children even when their response is minimal. 'You have been colouring in very carefully.'

- *Ask an open question:* if you sense the child would like to talk, ask an open question which makes no assumptions. 'What has been the best part?' 'How did you decide what to do?' 'Where did you get the idea for that?'

- *Give specific targeted praise:* respond to what children tell you with specific information on what you see as the strengths in what they are doing. This information helps to deepen children's insight into what they are doing. This is task-related feedback. General praise such as 'that's great', 'how clever of you', does not extend their understanding of what they are achieving and is of less lasting value.

- *Reframe negative self-talk to encourage confidence:* listen carefully to what children say. Do they focus on the negative, are they preoccupied with what they find difficult? Are they short on confidence and looking for inspiration? How can you help children to see a more positive view of what they are doing?

## Developing a child's strengths map

Children have a powerful inner drive which encourages them to gain and improve skills. They have a strong desire for autonomy which makes them want to achieve as much as they can through independently working towards their own goals. Helping children to discover and build their strengths gives them a strong sense of both competence and self-reliance. This creates an internal map of what is important for them and what they would like to do more of in future. I like to think of this as their strengths map. Whenever we give children positive feedback about achievements which are important to them we reinforce their confidence and self-esteem.

To discover their personal identity children need a balance between freedom and safe boundaries. Unfettered and unprotected freedom, while exhilarating to the child, also carries risks. There is the obvious risk of physical danger but what is more likely is the risk of failure and frustration as they attempt things they cannot achieve and receive little support or acknowledgement of their efforts. In contrast, a world which is overly controlled by well-intentioned adults risks over-protection which can stifle children's curiosity and restrict their chances to discover and build their strengths. This also leads to frustration along with a limited understanding of their strengths and capabilities.

What children need is a light touch, which encourages them to discover and build their strengths while offering a safety net to cushion the impact of any fall out when they over reach themselves. Encouraging children to talk becomes easier when you apply the positive communication principles in conjunction with appreciative attention.

# COMMUNICATION: RAPPORT, TRUST AND SHARING HOPES AND DREAMS

Once children are fluent communicators they need time to talk about what matters to them and to gain encouragement and support. They need to explore possibilities through sharing their goals and aspirations. Using language to plan and reflect encourages children to weigh up possibilities, to aspire to greater things and to decide how to make them happen. Hope and optimism are the life blood of growth and ambition and both need to be carefully nurtured to prevent a child becoming discouraged by setbacks or afraid of taking risks to work towards challenging goals.

Research into the nature of positive support explored how people listened and offered encouragement. Originally based on examining the dialogue between dating couples some interesting principles emerged about what supports people's aspirations and what crushes their enthusiasm. Shelly Gable and her colleagues from the University of California identified four types of response to good news, only one of which offers sincere and generous support (Figure 4).[39]

| Active and Constructive | Passive and Constructive |
|---|---|
| 'Wow, you got a merit in class today, tell me all about it. I want to know exactly what happened.' | 'Well done.' |
| | No attempt to build rapport or ask for further detail. Non- verbal signals may be restricted and hard to read. Child will be discouraged from talking. |
| Excellent rapport: positive non-verbal communication with warm tone of voice and smiling. This encourages child to offer further information. | |
| **Active and Destructive** | **Passive and Destructive** |
| 'What a shame you didn't get one for your science project. It proves what you can do when you work hard.' | 'Have you got much homework to do tonight?' |
| Communication at all levels is negative and hostile. Child is stopped in their tracks. | Avoids subject and non-verbal communication is evasive with limited eye contact. Child is left confused and unsure whether they have been heard. |

Figure 4: Four types of response to good news

Supporting young people when they share their good news or their hopes for the future gives them the back up they need to take on challenges. Most of us are aware of when we are in 'active and destructive' mode but it is easy when preoccupied to slip into the passive mode which denies the oxygen of enthusiasm that is needed to boost morale and recognize hopes and aspiration. A simple first step towards active and constructive responding is a 'no buts' rule. If you feel a 'but' coming on, it may suggest you are moving towards a critical rather than confirming role in the conversation. If you listen and actively support, you will be more likely to be asked for advice later and that would probably be a better time for the 'what if' questions.

Of course the active and constructive response is not just for adults. Young people will find their friendships will be more rewarding when they use this approach with their friends. Their relationships with adults will be less fraught too when they are more aware of how to respond to people. It can be funny and very instructive to role play the four different response patterns.

## SUMMARY

- A child's psychological wellbeing depends fundamentally on the quality of their relationships.

- The eight positive communication principles identify what creates rapport and trust for a child.

- Children learn about themselves from how others respond to them. Both appreciative attention and active and constructive responding techniques provide the ideal support to give children confidence in themselves.

- Activities to explore your own positive communication strengths will help you to identify what works best for you.

Factor 4

# Learning Strengths

## Developing Learning Habits
## to Motivate and Get Results

### Overview

In this section we will explore how to create the best conditions
for successful learning and examine the personal factors which
help a child to flourish.

- Find out why 'learning to learn' is an essential skill in a rapidly
  changing world.

- Discover why creativity is essential to both life satisfaction and
  adaptability.

- Learning how play is a foundation skill for creative, self-
  directed learning.

- Discover the importance of flow.

- Discover how a growth mindset assists successful learners.

- Explore why rewards are not always motivating.

- Evaluate whether to promote learning styles or learning
  strengths.

## LEARNING FOR LIFE

How can we help children to become independent and successful learners?
What do children need to know about themselves and the learning process so
they can adapt their behaviour, reflect on their needs and manage their own
learning to fit circumstances? How can children become versatile learners
able to develop new skills throughout life?

## Learning to learn

The rate of innovation and change has been breathtakingly rapid in the past century. Every aspect of domestic and working life has been changed by scientific and technological inventions. The rate of change has speeded up even more rapidly in the past 20 years. We can't predict what the next generation will need to know 25 years from now when the average 15-year-old will be in the middle of their working life. However, we can prepare them to become independent and successful learners, who are flexible and adaptable. Once they become adults, they will need to make decisions which are in their best interests or else risk being left adrift as the world changes around them. We need to help every child learn how to learn.

At the start of life, children are creative and independently minded, with the curiosity and energy to drive their enthusiasm. People who are successful and satisfied with their lives seem to retain this passion and creativity. To explore how children can become successful learners, we need to know what helps and what hinders them from becoming skilled and enthusiastic in the pursuit of knowledge. The foundation skills are laid very early, well before children attend school, so it is helpful to understand the essential building blocks of learning, formed in the first few years. Learning is a social process and the infant's experience of sharing and communication within the family has a lasting impact.

## Developing a mind of your own

In their first two to three years children become increasingly aware of themselves and others and able to communicate and ask questions. The quality of their experience and the warmth they experience from adults shapes how they approach learning. To become happy, confident and successful learners children need opportunities to do the following:

- *Tune into people as a source of fun and information:* the more closely attuned parents are to the child's interests, the more zest and energy the child shows for exploring and hands on learning.

- *Listen and learn about language:* how quickly a child develops vocabulary is related to parental responsiveness. It is not a matter of how many words the child hears around them, but more the number of exchanges between the child and the adult and how effectively the adult responds to what has caught the child's attention.

- *Imitate what they see others doing:* once children have some control of their limbs and the sounds they can make, they start to enjoy games where they take turns with someone. The babble games and arm waving that babies initially enjoy gradually develops into following adults around to imitate what they are doing.

- *Communicate their own interests:* while copying others can be fun, children have a strong sense of what they want to explore and try out for themselves. The family which encourages this, while ensuring the toddler is safe from harm, is providing the ideal environment for a child to begin to discover and develop their strengths.

- *Starting and sustaining play:* from around 18 months old children's play becomes more deliberate, as they begin to remember how things work and begin to experiment to find out more. They can join things together and gradually become more adept with making things. Children start to create things and see the impact.

- *Develop fantasy play and use their imagination:* a child's experiences coupled with their improving memory and language skills stimulate creativity and innovation. The child now definitely has a mind of their own.

## Compensatory experience

Missing out on a rich and varied early experience need not be a permanent disadvantage for children. We know that children adopted after spending time in orphanages, such as those in Romania in the 1980s, did make significant progress post-adoption. The human brain is adaptable, and can make up for missed experience, but each stage of development is important and necessary. Children who have had a narrow or restricted experience of the world may need to revisit earlier stages of development and consolidate each stage before they can move forward.

## THE FIVE LEARNING SUCCESS SKILLS
### Creating happy, confident and successful learners

In the first three years the foundations for successful learning are established. Children gain essential experience through exploring their environment. Their experience through play builds a rich picture of the world. The five key skill areas together provide children with the essential tools for early learning which, once established, will give them confidence and motivation (Figure 5).

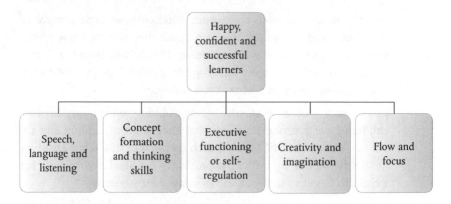

Figure 5: The five learning success skills

## 1. Speech, language and listening

The first, and possibly the best understood, skill, which underpins successful learning is language. It is a vital all round skill which children need to think and understand themselves, as well as to communicate with others. Language abilities develop rapidly in the first three years and allow children to make sense of their world. In the previous chapter, we explored the power of positive communication and how it impacts on the child's development.

As language skills develop, this allows the child both to understand and be understood. At the same time, physical coordination is becoming more fluent, which produces greater mobility and eye–hand coordination, enabling the child to explore and handle things around them. This greater volume of experience needs to be managed, so that it is not fragmented and chaotic.

Language has a central role in organizing experience. The child's ability to make sense of the information taken in through all their senses is hugely assisted by naming objects and actions. The child's memory for people and events also becomes more reliable. The next important step is to learn how all these objects and experiences are connected to each other.

## 2. Concept formation and thinking skills

It is an important core skill to recognize and name individual objects and actions, but as the child's knowledge grows so does the need to connect them into categories. Concept formation – how things relate to each other – begins to develop in parallel with language. It is a huge step forward, and is vital for making sense of experience. This process impacts on all areas of development including language, perception, thinking and movement. It makes it possible for the child to recognize things which belong together, although they may look dissimilar. A child learns to recognize not just their own drinking cup, but all cups, and not just the family dog, but gradually the concept of dogs and then of animals.

Concept formation, or categorization, streamlines learning and makes it adaptable to new situations and new examples. This is in itself a mammoth task, and for the first three years at least it is as if the child is building their knowledge library, one section at a time and cataloguing what they find. It is no surprise that young children can't multi-task. Imagine visiting a supermarket which holds a huge range of goods but does not display them according to any system you can recognize. Not only would shopping take much longer but it would be most confusing and stressful. You would become tired and frustrated, and you might even want to shout or cry. Welcome to a small child's world. Young children do find the world as confusing as this disorganized shop. This explains why it is not unusual for children to get tetchy and frustrated when they are in a busy environment. Routine, in itself a form of categorization, brings an order and certainty to what is about to happen. Unsurprisingly, routine is often recommended as the key to creating a calmer life when you have a small child.

## 3. Executive functioning or self-regulation

A baby can only concentrate on one thing at a time but gradually, over the next two to three years, a child begins to make more sense of the world and is in a stronger position to plan and make choices. What happens next allows the child to move on from episodic and fragmented learning, where each experience is laboriously categorized piece by piece, to a more recognizable and better understood experience. Around the age of three the child enters the next big stage, as the control centre for learning begins to mature in the frontal lobe of the brain. This enables the child to integrate and coordinate knowledge – becoming capable of what psychologists call *executive function* or, sometimes, *self-regulation*.

This 'control centre' manages all the complex cognitive skills like attention, thinking and memory which are required when we do anything that is not automatic or routine. It allows us to over-ride impulses and distractions to stay on task. It is also used for problem solving or developing complex tasks. The control and coordination of cognitive skills is a complex process which takes many years of practice and refinement throughout childhood. However, its emergence makes a significant difference to what children are able to do. Imagine trying to hold a conversation in a busy cafe if you could not screen out what other people were saying at the next table. We sometimes take our ability to focus and screen out distractions for granted but young children cannot easily do this. Even more frustrating would be trying to manage deceptively simple but actually complex tasks like making a cup of tea if you could only remember one or two parts of the required sequence.

A baby starts life having great difficulty filtering out what psychologist and philosopher William James called the 'booming, buzzing confusion' of a stimulus-rich world.[40] As children grow towards the pre-school years they learn first to categorize information and then to plan and organize sequences of actions. This is important progress. How well these skills develop makes a huge difference to children, improving their ability to get involved in any task in the first place and strengthening their ability to persist until they have achieved the final outcome. This is vital to enable children to learn and flourish. Until recently, theories about pre-school education considered the development of executive function as an incidental outcome of early experience. Now it is recognized as a crucial driver for learning.

## 4. Creativity and imagination

Children learn about the world through play. Play is exciting, absorbing and an extremely effective way to learn. However, there has been a tendency to assume it is a temporary element of development, an early stage which is outgrown in favour of more formal teaching and learning. This may be a serious mistake which deprives children of play, the fundamental source of creativity.

Children gain a sense of autonomy and competence early on through play which absorbs and engages their interest. There are no rights and wrongs in play and the child is able to experiment and be creative. Children engage in play spontaneously without seeking adult encouragement or rewards. Independent play is also an essential stepping stone for learning how to plan, organize and maintain focus on a task. Play keeps a child's interest and by sustaining their attention play gradually helps a child develop all the skills which underpin executive function. This vital command and control centre of the brain which plans and monitors what is happening will be essential once the child starts school.

Play is fun but it also helps build important thinking and learning skills. While children are doing something that excites them, like building a Lego model, they are also learning to focus attention, ignore distractions and plan the steps they need to complete the project. Spontaneous play like this is creative and unstructured, allowing the child independence to plan, explore and adapt according to what they find. Play which is structured, as in a set game organized by an adult or the use of a specific toy, does not offer all the same advantages. Although 'playing with' a toy can hold a child's attention, if the specific demands of the toy or game are predetermined it will not call upon the same breadth of cognitive skills and planning as independent play.

### 5. Flow and focus

Children gradually learn to focus their attention and sustain what they are doing until they are satisfied with the outcome. When children become fluent in doing this via something they enjoy, they experience flow. Flow is a state of absorption and engagement which sustains effort and involvement. Nature offers a perfect route into flow through independent play, enabling the child to choose something that interests them, and then become fully absorbed. However, the challenge for young children is that their skills are restricted, and they may not be able to complete something as planned. The frustration this causes is often a big barrier for a young child. Young children can't easily do what they want to do for themselves, so they either give up, or seek something less challenging. However, as we shall see later, adult-supported play will provide the scaffolding that children need to achieve their plans successfully.

## HOW ADULTS CAN HELP CHILDREN BECOME CONFIDENT AND INDEPENDENT LEARNERS

Play can give children a sense of control and direction which encourages them to use their strengths. However, a young child's play frequently meets hurdles which they cannot get over. Often children become frustrated when they run out of ideas and will abandon what they are doing and move on to something else, unless adult support is there to help them find a way forward. Playing at the limit of your knowledge and experience is both frustrating and less effective than adult-supported play which gently adds a little stretch. Young children's difficulty with categorizing and sequencing means their experience can be chaotic and gentle pointers to identify how things go together can help children create their own mental maps. This is not the adult teaching the child, but rather acting as a play assistant to help the child stay on track.

## Scaffolding learning

The process of helping children to inch forward with adult support to 'scaffold' their learning was first described by Lev Vygotsky.[37] His work suggests that children reach sticking points, within the existing boundaries of their knowledge and competence unless adults can help them move forward. Vygotsky referred to these sticking points as *zones of proximal development*. He was the first to identify an important dynamic between the child and the adult, in the distinction he makes between formal teaching, which is not effective with young children, and 'scaffolding' which supports the child to make their own discoveries.

The young child who is working at the limits of their knowledge may only need a small pointer to make that leap of understanding. The supporting adult may just need to direct their attention at the right time and place to move them on little by little without taking over control. Play provides the zest and enthusiasm to learn while sensitively managed adult support gives the child the impetus to move forward.

# MOTIVATION AND SUCCESS: ENCOURAGING A ZEST4LEARNING

No one would deny that a good school plays a significant role in a child's life but the attitudes and skills a child contributes to the mix are vitally important. The step up from pre-school to school is a significant one, which depends upon more than just the development and maturity of cognitive skills as the basis for learning. For much of the twentieth century, the emphasis in learning research was on exploring intelligence as the factor that predicts educational progress. This single-factor view of success has proved to be incomplete and a range of 'soft' factors are known to have equal impact. Motivation is the factor which determines whether children fulfil their potential or whether they underperform.

A zest for learning is highly personal and separate from intelligence. There is a chain reaction of four interlinked factors which impact on success (Figure 6).

1. *Emotional wellbeing* is the first factor which underpins motivation. When a child is emotionally secure they can manage negative feelings without becoming overwhelmed by them. A child who is calm and confident is well placed to engage with new experiences. Emotional wellbeing anchors the ability to learn. Children who are not comfortable with themselves, and who are unsure of their place in the

world, find it hard to settle and engage with learning. The emotional area of the brain, when left in a switched-on state for long periods, upsets the biochemistry of the brain required for concentration and learning. It particularly affects the development of the planning and organizing part of the brain which manages concentrated effort. The impact of emotional wellbeing on learning is now widely accepted in schools with both local and central government initiatives available to help schools promote emotional wellbeing.

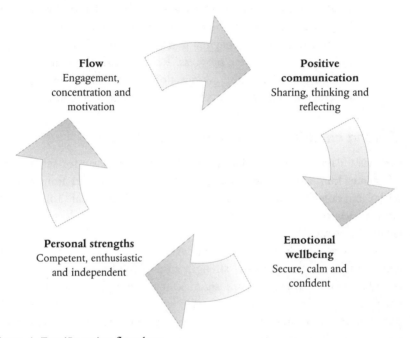

**Flow**
Engagement, concentration and motivation

**Positive communication**
Sharing, thinking and reflecting

**Personal strengths**
Competent, enthusiastic and independent

**Emotional wellbeing**
Secure, calm and confident

Figure 6: Zest4Learning flowchart

2. A calmer, more confident outlook enables the child to explore and use their *personal strengths* which brings a deep satisfaction, a sense of competence and an enthusiasm for exploring new experiences. Self Determination Theory shows us that self-motivated learning requires opportunities for autonomy, competence and positive relationships to support progress. Children who know their strengths and who are encouraged to use them have a profound sense of their own competence and future potential.

3. The experience of competence and mastery builds a child's enthusiasm for play and later makes the discovery of *flow* more likely. Experiencing flow appears to be essential for achieving high performance as it sustains the effort required for the many hours of practice to gain expertise, for example, learning to read.

4. This virtuous circle provided by the first three factors is finally consolidated by *positive communication* skills which give a child a firm grounding in developing trust and asking for adult support. Children who are confident learners engage well with their teachers. They have a well-established range of behaviours which support and consolidate learning. They enjoy talking about what they are doing and reflecting on their progress. Reflection deepens and develops thinking skills. They also ask questions to help them solve a problem and are more likely to actively contribute to group work.

## Helping children to find their Zest4Learning

Let's visit Toby again. Toby had definitely lost enthusiasm for school when I first met him. He was not lacking in ability or in support from home or school but somehow this was not connecting with the 'real' Toby to draw out his enthusiasm and engagement with learning. Toby was lost and needed to find his way.

Toby was already a keen creative writer so the solution came through connecting with this personal strength in a playful way which gave him confidence and sparked his enthusiasm. Our starting point was Toby's vivid imagination, and his enjoyment of exciting plots with plenty of action. He didn't need any prompting to write these stories and they often emerged from creative day dreaming that happily occupied his free time. He also enjoyed fantasy play with models he had made. Toby enjoyed spending time inside his head and his stories were an attempt to capture that play experience.

This style of writing was radically different from the formal writing activities in lessons. Toby found it difficult to organize his thoughts around the subject set by his teacher for the class. He also needed to focus on spelling, vocabulary and grammar. Taking a sideways step to allow Toby to do more free writing remotivated him to write. At first his attempts were rather simple, focusing on the sequence of events and with only limited description. Gradually he began to experiment with words and to imagine how his stories would sound when read aloud.

What had started as an extension of his play undoubtedly benefited from his natural motivation to practise and improve. He started to take a greater interest in the building blocks of language and the literacy lessons began to bring both his use of grammar and vocabulary to life. Because he was able to read to younger children occasionally he now had a purpose for writing more effectively. He no longer saw writing as solely valuable for capturing his vivid fantasies, but also now realized it was a way to connect with an audience. Over time Toby became able to write in a broader range of styles. He became less reliant on the feedback from his young audience and more confident of his own writing style.

## Home school/partnership, building Zest4Learning

If the key to happy confident and successful learning lies in the 'soft factors' which create a zest for learning then we need to factor in both the child and the home into any consideration about raising standards of education. While how teachers teach is monumentally important, it is a big subject and not the focus of this book. However, what the special ingredients of a supportive home actually are is highly pertinent. How do we deconstruct 'the supportive home' into its component parts, and when we have done that what does it tell us about what the child brings to learning as a result of this support. I would suggest that the four facets of the Zest4Learning model summarize that positive advantage. All these areas have a strong evidence base for their importance in promoting wellbeing and preparedness for learning. Where families need support to promote the child's engagement with learning then there are a range of strategies schools can use to good effect.

## Spreading the Zest4Learning message

### DROP-IN SESSIONS AND OPEN MORNINGS

Many parents have fragmented memories of education which is not always happy. They may find it hard to know how to encourage and facilitate learning and may remember harsh and critical feedback. Seeing school in a different light at a drop-in session, for instance, is an important first step.

### PARENT COURSES

The popular notion of parent courses is that they are designed to manage a child's behaviour and are aimed at parents who aren't coping. However, many parenting programmes are more ambitious than this and are designed to help parents support their child's emotional wellbeing and teach skills and techniques to create positive communication, central to the Zest4Learning approach.

### SUBJECT WORKSHOPS

These initially help parents understand how a subject is taught in the school and how to support this at home but they also serve to encourage identifying and building a child's strengths if this is an area of interest to them.

### PARENT EVENINGS

Not only a chance to give a progress report on educational attainments, parent evenings also provide time to discuss what enthuses each child and how their strengths can be identified and used effectively both at school and at home.

### EXTRACURRICULAR ACTIVITIES

The art, the sport, the singing and the dance and drama are still sometimes seen as the frills which add a little light relief, but are of marginal value to education. However, each and all of these build personal qualities which enrich a child's capacity to learn. Children gain social and communication skills through working with others and also learn to manage and organize themselves effectively. It is not surprising that both university entrance and graduate employers often look first at the personal qualities contained in an application.

## BRINGING OUT THE BEST IN EACH CHILD: THE 3M FORMULA FOR SUCCESS

There is an increasing awareness of the importance of personalized learning but the details of how to make this a reality for all children needs fleshing out. Parents and professionals need the tools to identify a child's strengths and to create an environment which addresses the whole child's needs. We need clarity on how personalized learning works in practice to bring out the best in each child, particularly when a child is vulnerable and underperforming.

How might we translate personalized learning into practice both at home and at school? What if a child has not fully established the building blocks for learning so that their core skills of language, thinking, executive functioning, creativity and imagination along with flow are still at a rudimentary stage? How can you move them forward? What can you do to help another child who has these skills but remains disengaged without the Zest4Learning provided by emotional wellbeing, positive communication skills, personal strengths and the ability to achieve flow? Where do you start to cultivate their enthusiasm and nurture their self-belief? The answer lies in the support you can provide on three vital fronts which encourages a positive mindset for learning, and which nurtures motivation via sensitive and supportive mentoring. In short the 3M formula for success: mindset, motivation and mentoring.

Ability is much more than the traditional concept of intelligence would suggest. The emphasis on intelligence as the key to success encourages a fatalistic view that 'you either have it or you don't'. Generations of parents and professionals have assumed that intelligence is inborn, stable over time and not easily influenced. Research in recent years has focused on the application of ability and has reminded us that it is 'not what you have got but how you use it' that makes all the difference.

## Supporting children's learning

Children need support to learn how to be effective learners. They need to 'learn to learn'. Supporting children's learning has gone through a number of phases over the years. Initially it was assumed that 'study skills' techniques played a major part in successful learning by ensuring you committed what you had been taught effectively to memory ready for examination. Children were taught how to take notes and how to improve their memory in preparation for exams. More recently the focus has moved away from how well students 'catch and keep' the curriculum to looking at individual differences in how children approach learning. Various models of learning style have been proposed to capture the differences in how people approach learning. Some models of learning style look solely at perceptual differences: whether you pay most attention to visual or auditory information or whether you need to be more actively involved. A number of other models look at how you think and organize material. People were encouraged to identify and develop children's learning styles but this has not been backed up by strong research evidence about effectiveness.[41]

What galvanizes effective personalized learning is helping children to develop their learning strengths. Earlier we looked at the 20 prime strengths which give children a start on the road to personalized learning. Alongside an independent experience of discovering and developing their strengths, every child needs adult guidance to nurture the 3M formula for success: mindset, motivation and mentoring (Figure 7). This provides the positive and optimistic energy a child needs to enjoy and engage with learning.

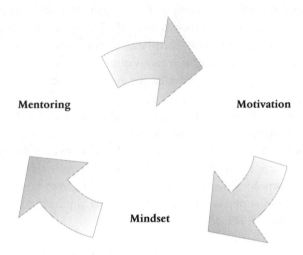

Figure 7: The 3M formula

## 1. Mindset

How you think about learning profoundly influences what you do. Carol Dweck's research has shown that success is not down to innate ability alone.[42] Her research in schools across the United States has illustrated how mindset powerfully influences the learning process. She has shown that what children believe about the nature of ability profoundly affects their engagement with learning, their persistence when faced with challenge and their willingness to take risks and make mistakes. Dweck describes two contrasting mindsets – the fixed ability and the growth mindset – and their impact on learning (Table 2).

Table 2: The features of the two mindsets

| Fixed ability mindset | Growth mindset |
| --- | --- |
| 1. Learning ability is fixed by intelligence | 1. Learning is driven by effort |
| 2. Mistakes result from personal limitations | 2. Mistakes are part of learning |
| 3. Progress depends on outside help | 3. Progress comes with practice |
| 4. Speed of learning is a sign of ability | 4. Slow and careful gets there |
| 6. Learning strategies are just technique | 5. Persistence often pays off |
| 6. Practice merely polishes performance | 6. Practice can lead to breakthroughs |
| 7. I have limited control over results | 7. I have significant control over results |

## THE FIXED ABILITY MINDSET

This view is linked to traditional concepts of intelligence. When children believe that the ability to learn is a capacity with fixed limits, this affects what they do when faced with a challenge. If they cannot easily find a solution, they are likely to assume they have reached their ceiling of ability and will either withdraw or ask for help. If they regularly meet challenges in a subject, they may then tell themselves that they lack ability in this area and may in future avoid further involvement or lower their expectations. This creates a cycle of low effort and a focus on seeking external solutions. Children assume that they are the problem and discount the importance of either gaining more experience or increasing practice levels. They are even less likely to try to identify effective problem solving strategies. Interestingly much of Dweck's research has been focused on children's mastery of mathematical skills, which depend on a combination of learning facts and developing creative problem solving skills. A fixed mindset is a distinct disadvantage in this subject where persistence and experimentation often lead to breakthroughs to a higher level of understanding.

## THE GROWTH MINDSET

When a child is encouraged to believe that learning is an ability which improves with practice, the outcomes are very different. Learning to apply effort and developing a set of useful problem solving techniques gives a child confidence and a sense of control when facing a challenge. The challenge is seen as a practical issue rather than a personal one. Carol Dweck describes children in the growth mindset group who respond with 'I love a challenge,' while the refrain of the fixed ability group was 'I'm no good at this'. Learners who think of ability as similar to a muscle, which strengthens with practice, are going to be comfortable with exploring and using strategies which develop their problem solving skills. The hallmarks of a growth mindset are effort and persistence which increase the time spent engaged with a task and which in turn increases the experience that they subsequently gain. Time spent practising a skill is, unsurprisingly, strongly associated with success.

## HOW SELF-EFFICACY AFFECTS PERFORMANCE

The common factor which explains these two contrasting mindsets is 'self-efficacy'. This psychological concept identifies how a positive and optimistic belief about your competence and skill in any area strongly influences your likelihood of success. If you believe you have control over the results, and are optimistic about your likelihood of success, you are more likely both to get involved with a task and to persist when it is not straightforward. This is self-efficacy. Children with low self-efficacy have a pessimistic view of the likelihood of their success. They tend to avoid tasks when they can, or disengage quickly when the challenge becomes apparent. Dweck's research is particularly useful in reminding us that many children can have just such a narrow view of themselves as learners. When a child's view of their intelligence is dominated by a fixed ability mindset, the child assumes the factors influencing success are not within their control. In contrast, if a child is encouraged to develop a growth mindset they will be confident of being in control and feel optimistic about taking action.

## HOW TO HELP A CHILD DEVELOP A GROWTH MINDSET

Adults who make a real difference to a child's life offer two gifts of lifelong value. The first gift is to help a child to believe that they have huge potential to learn and are capable and competent. To give this gift, the adult acts like a mirror reflecting back the good, the optimistic and the useful things that they notice. This helps a child to be aware of what they can do and of the promise of continuing improvement as they go along.

The second gift is to ensure a significant degree of freedom so that the child can make choices and discover what they are capable of. Adult support assists but does not control their efforts. What a child believes about their capacity to learn makes the difference between firing on all cylinders, and moving along slowly and spasmodically, uncertain of direction or destination. A growth mindset determines how you make sense of your experience of learning. You believe that learning is a skill that you can practise and that challenges can be faced squarely with the right tools and support.

Martin Seligman, in his book *The Optimistic Child*, describes an essential set of beliefs or 'explanatory style' which each of us takes into any situation.[43] There are three key components of explanatory style: whether you believe the outcomes of an action are *permanent, personal* or *pervasive*. Each of these elements can be negative or positive, internal or external.

Let's look at what this might mean for a class of nine-year-olds who take a science test, as we meet Josh, Emma, Gary and Lara. They are all disappointed with the results of their test, but each child explains the outcome differently:

- *Josh* admits he didn't spend enough time studying – his explanatory style is *personal* but not permanent or pervasive. He expects to do better next time, now that he is aware of what would help him improve. He is upset with himself but only on a temporary basis.

- *Emma* is adamant that it is not her fault. She says the teacher is boring and science does not interest her. She is going to work in fashion one day where art is more important. Emma's explanatory style is *external* – focused on her teacher and the subject, so it does not impact on her self-belief.

- *Gary* is very upset. He wanted to do well but has struggled with his science lessons. He has believed for some time that he lacks ability, and therefore has been too embarrassed to ask his teacher or his parents for help. He has withdrawn from being actively involved in lessons and has developed low expectations. Gary has a *negative*, pessimistic explanatory style where he thinks the situation is *permanent, personal* and *pervasive*. Unless he gains the confidence to seeks help he will need an astute adult to recognise his beliefs are creating a problem. Otherwise it is likely that he will spiral downwards in a self-fulfilling prophecy of failure. Gary is highly vulnerable to anxiety, and feelings of failure and low self-worth.

- *Lauren* is also very upset. She is an articulate girl who has strong literacy skills but is less confident with the more analytical approach required in science. She was keen to do well and tried hard. Her explanatory style is *personal* and specific to science but not *permanent*. Lauren's parents have encouraged a growth mindset by talking about learning as something you learn how to do. Unfortunately this well-intentioned advice is rather abstract and Lauren hasn't been shown any practical approaches which would help her in science. Her teacher has overestimated Lauren's skills in science and says things like 'just do your best' and 'you are a clever girl, I know you can work it out for yourself.' Adult expectations for Lauren are positive, optimistic but not realistic or practical. Lauren needs specific and detailed support to assist her own efforts. There is an individualized programme designed specifically for Lauren at the end of this chapter.

## 2. Motivation

Motivation describes the energy, enthusiasm and persistence which help to sustain you as you work towards goals. When you are highly motivated you take regular and sustained action to make something happen. If your motivation is low, you may prefer to talk about something a lot but do very little. You may be easily distracted or take avoiding action. Motivation can either be generated externally and dependent on praise or rewards or it can be self-determined and driven by personal goals.

Exploring what best motivates a child will give you a starting point both to encourage short-term success and to help children develop greater self-efficacy. While adults generally agree about the importance of encouraging of self-motivation, knowing how to help children to become self-motivated is less well understood. There is also some doubt about how best to use rewards to encourage children without undermining their own self-reliance.

Self-motivation is more likely to develop when children have a growth mindset because both come from the same belief that you have the control and competence to gain success. Getting to the position where you believe that about yourself requires time and experience. Motivation is not inborn and is greatly influenced by the experiences adults offer to children.

### ENCOURAGING SELF-MOTIVATED LEARNING

Children naturally approach the world with curiosity and a desire to explore. They want to gain competence and will strive through their play to master a range of skills.

Deci and Ryan's Self Determination Theory, which helps us understand how personal strengths develop, identifies autonomy and competence as two of the three key drivers of positive wellbeing.[44] The third driver is relatedness, what is commonly understood as a sense of belonging and being valued. Adult support to help a child learn provides that third element, particularly in the form of specific and targeted praise and feedback.

### ARE REWARDS ALWAYS REWARDING?

Research into the effect of rewards suggests that how effective rewards are in improving performance depends on the type of task. When the task is dull or routine, a reward can be an advantage in sustaining effort and encouraging a speedier response to an activity which would otherwise gradually slow down.

However, where an activity is creative or requires careful thought, rewards seem to have the opposite effect. Performance is often impaired by direct rewards. Where innovation and creativity are required people respond best to having the time and opportunity to get deeply involved. Rewards seem to undermine self-motivation and interfere with the development of flow – that intense and prolonged ability to stay focused on any activity which is personally important and satisfying.

## FINDING FLOW

Activities which naturally encourage flow are art, music and dancing, but it can be experienced in any area of life where we are fully and completely involved, doing something for its own sake, because we want to and because we have a burning desire to take it to the next level and expand our skill. Flow gives the energy and commitment to do something with grit and persistence. Flow is not about always feeling happy and entranced by what you are doing. Sometimes we struggle to move on and have to call upon 'stick-with-it' skills. At other times, things are going so well, we are totally into what we are doing and self-awareness is so subsumed that we don't even spend time thinking about whether we are happy.

## FLOW AND SUCCESS

Learning complex skills requires flow. Becoming a highly skilled musician, artist or athlete requires dogged determination and consistent, intensive, often daily practice. You could do it as a mindless slog, or because your mother made you practise, but in the end you will rebel if your heart is not in it. Anders Ericsson completed a study at the Berlin Academy of Music with violin students.[45] Their teachers had rated them into three groups: the stars with world class soloist potential, the 'good' group who had professional concert potential and those unlikely to play professionally. When they were interviewed, it was not how early they had started to play, but how intensively they had practised which differentiated the groups. By the age of 20 the elite performers had clocked up 10,000 hours of practice.

Flow is a positive and important practical outcome of self-motivated learning. Children who experience flow, gain deep satisfaction from the process of learning itself, and are more likely to engage in future with activities which lead to flow. Toys and games which produce their own reward either on completion, or in the case of electronic games at regular intervals, can interfere with flow. These rewards are often the appeal of the game. Children play in order to be rewarded rather than enjoying the process of play itself.

## BUILDING AND SUPPORTING MOTIVATION

You will know that children are self-motivated when:

- they plan and organize what they need to get started
- there is a personal goal which they can identify
- work progresses with little prompting
- work continues for extended periods without breaks
- they will ask for help when needed but prefer to be independent
- they gain personal satisfaction from outcomes.

You will know that children are reward dependent when:

- a clear structure and routine is needed to support organized work
- they are not clear on the purpose of the task
- high levels of praise and feedback are needed to sustain involvement
- work is focused on outcomes rather than enjoying the process
- they may give in easily when facing a challenge
- they show little sign of satisfaction in the task.

Tasks which benefit from rewards are:

- repetitive tasks requiring practice which may seem dull, e.g. multiplication tables
- tasks where the relevance to the child is unclear
- tasks which are too difficult for the child to complete confidently and fluently
- any task which the child really dislikes.

To encourage self-motivation:

- make the purpose of the activity clear: both what is involved in carrying out the task and what it will teach the child as a result
- encourage children to set personal goals which are positively phrased 'I will…' to reinforce a sense of growing competence

- ensure children review their progress and adjust goals as required
- encourage children to compete against themselves rather than to look at what their peers are doing
- divide tasks into small, achievable steps to guarantee success
- give children some independence to plan the process to encourage a sense of autonomy
- encourage children to see the support you offer as a form of progress review not something which results from mistakes or poor performance
- ensure positive feedback which is specific and informative to help a child understand what is working well. Ideally this should be up to five times more frequent than improvement suggestions.

## 3. Mentoring

Children have three ways of assessing their progress when they are learning a new skill:

- *Their own sense of progress*, which is often unreliable because of their inexperience and lack of standards for comparison.
- How much *task satisfaction* they gain, which is fragile because of the nature of learning which is fraught with challenges and frustrations.
- *How adults respond* to their efforts. When the adult focuses on what is going well and comments positively on the effort that has led to gaining success children receive a strong message about their personal competence. This encourages them to feel in control and interested in doing more. In contrast, when the adult identifies areas in need of improvement or suggests alterations children lose their sense of independence and mastery.

Given that children are always powerfully aware of how much they still have to learn they can become easily discouraged. Offering support which is informative as well as encouraging is a delicate balancing act.

I use the word mentoring because it describes how support is given, and in what spirit, rather than who is doing the mentoring. Mentoring has recently become semi-professionalized as something people do who join youth projects or who work one to one in schools. I'd like to broaden that out to see mentoring as a skill set available for any, and hopefully all, adults to adopt when supporting children and young people.

## LIGHTING THE FIRE: SUPPORTING CHILDREN TO LEARN

Michelangelo's letters describe his first love, sculpture, as the act of revealing what already lies within the marble. This rather modest notion, that his genius lay in seeing the potential of a block of marble, does, in fact, beautifully describe the powerful ability of the artist to bring something original to life.

No two children are the same, and the seeds of their potential are there, waiting for the right conditions to allow them to flourish. Releasing that potential is, in no small part, about helping a child to find their zest for learning. Children need a strong self-belief which will energize and drive their own efforts. The child's capacity for wellbeing depends upon being part of an understanding world which cherishes and nurtures their individual strengths. They need encouragement to become active, curious and self-motivated.

No child is a blank slate waiting to be drawn upon by others; nor is the 'inner child' able to make its own way out into the world fully revealed and polished to perfection. Children are deeply dependent on adults to set the stage, to allow them to discover who they are, explore what they are capable of and encourage them to make their unique contribution to the world.

## WHAT MAKES A GOOD MENTOR?

- Warmth and rapport – children quickly sense when you have their best interests at heart and believe in them.

- Emotional sensitivity, so that you can detect, acknowledge and calm fears and uncertainties.

- Positive communication skills to draw out the child's views and to encourage them to think and ask questions.

- Asking open questions, which encourages the child to reflect and form an independent view.

- Empathy – to see the world through the child's eyes and understand their perspective.

- Respect for the child – an unconditional acceptance of them as they are, whatever their challenges are now.

- Optimism, which sustains belief in a good future when times get tough.

- Vision for the future, giving a powerful sense of the possibilities for change.

- Enthusiasm, to help make a dull subject interesting and worthwhile.

- Encouraging autonomy, but providing safe boundaries so that the child feels secure and protected.

- Positivity, which helps to reframe a negative experience and find positive solutions.

- Creativity, to make a task interesting, relevant and exciting.

- Being a good role model: demonstrating how to act with optimism, energy, generosity, commitment.

- Openness about your personal strengths and how they contribute to your own wellbeing. Children like to know what matters to you and how you manage challenges.

## PUTTING THE 3MS INTO PRACTICE

Lauren's result in the science test surprised everyone. Her family and school agreed to work together to build her confidence and practical skills. They agreed to a number of strategies designed to build her strengths and support her learning. Lauren had definite strengths in her love of language and her communication skills but her social maturity and eagerness to please had encouraged people to overestimate her independence when facing challenges.

### Boosting creativity and imagination through daily time to play

Lauren's family agreed to make sure she had some time every day to follow her own interests and use her strengths. She was encouraged to choose what to do. The aim was to build her imagination and creativity which would also improve her attention span. Lauren found it easier to concentrate when choosing something interesting. This set the ideal conditions for her to experience flow enabling her to lose track of time and be able to focus on what she was doing without adult help. She had at least an hour a day for free play. This helped her to manage her own time and be independent. Her concentration span at school also increased and the standard of her work improved. She also became more independent, showing initiative in her work, rather than looking for detailed guidance from her teacher.

Successful learning is self-managed and, although teachers can inspire and inform, they cannot not supervise each learning step. Play is therefore important as the foundation for work. It's also fun and it does you good.

## Work with the child's strengths and abilities

Lauren had a unique combination of abilities and it is rare to be good at everything. Family and teachers were asked to note what she enjoyed doing.

The Prime Strengths Finder assessment tool can be used to pinpoint a child's emerging strengths. Lauren's strengths in language and communication suggested she should do more paired work in science so she and her partner could discuss and review work in progress. Lauren found that describing what she was doing and forming questions to ask helped her understand the process of designing a fair test and looking for evidence. She enjoyed being able to use her strengths in this way.

## Developing a growth mindset

Lauren was unsure of her abilities and unclear how she could influence events. She wondered whether other people were more naturally good at science. She saw challenges and mistakes as threats to her self-image which sets off a stress reaction which made it harder still. She was encouraged to see learning as a form of growth. The more you do the better you get. Then she could celebrate each step on the road to success. This optimistic view gave her confidence.

## Setting realistic goals

Attitude alone would not move Lauren forward; she needed realistic goals where she could see how she was making progress. Learning is like a series of small stepping stones to cross a river rather than a steep hill to climb. School and family became more realistic about what Lauren could do, based on her age and interests.

## Using the child's personal strengths and interests set the pace

Relevance is hugely important to progress; Lauren needed a stronger connection to topics so that she had ways of linking her new knowledge with her existing interests and understanding. The family used her interest in animals and their care as a launch pad into studying healthy living.

## See mistakes as signposts not problems

Lauren did not like to get things wrong, she worried about disappointing people. She was reassured that mistakes show us how we are doing so far. Mistakes provide information on where to go next. They are signposts for learning not roadblocks. Children with a growth mindset can learn to welcome them as challenges. Children with a fixed ability mindset see them as proof that they have reached their limits. One view creates energy, the other is draining.

## Praise effort not achievements

The driving force for success is effort and persistence. Lauren was regularly praised for her commitment and for the approach she has taken. She was given specific positive feedback not just on outcomes but on how she went about a task. How had she planned it? Was she well organized? How did she find ways around a problem? This was as useful when doing ordinary tasks at home, like tidying the bedroom or packing a school bag. She was praised for getting involved and trying to do things for herself.

## Turn negatives into positives

When Lauren got stuck or discouraged she was shown how to flip an idea to find the solution. If, for example, she said 'It's no good I can't remember,' she was encouraged to think what did help her to remember things well. She could then decide what to do to make it easier another time. Lauren likes drawing pictures and found that mind maps made connections which helped her to remember.

The key to learning success for Lauren was finding practical steps which both supported her difficulties and encouraged her strengths. By finding what worked, she not only improved her performance in school but also found the process more satisfying. Learning no longer seemed like hard work and drudgery but now was more relevant, accessible and achievable.

Now that Lauren knows she can be successful, she is more likely to continue to try, whatever the setback. She enjoys exploring and using interesting ways to learn and practise. She wants to learn and appreciates encouragement and support from teachers, friends and family. She feels confident about herself and the future.

## SUMMARY

- Successful learning depends more upon a number of practical factors that enable a child to learn effectively than it does on a fixed intellectual ability. These 'soft factors' need to be cultivated and nurtured to enable a child to 'learn to learn'.

- There are five core skill areas essential for successful learning:

  1. speech, language and listening

  2. concept formation and thinking skills

  3. executive functioning or self-regulation

  4. creativity and imagination

  5. flow and focus.

- All these five skill areas depend on socially supported learning and experience for which the mentoring approach is ideal both for parents and professionals.

- Children who have these core skills are more likely to be receptive to both independent learning and guided learning at home and at school.

- Ultimately we want children to have a self-driven Zest4Learning which comes from:

  1. emotional wellbeing

  2. personal strengths

  3. flow

  4. positive communication.

- The 3M formula – mindset, motivation and mentoring – explores how to support those children who need help to establish themselves as lifelong learners.

Factor 5

# Resilience

## How to Avoid Roadblocks and Bounce Back from Setbacks

### Overview

Resilience helps a child to:

- make good choices to avoid potentially damaging temptations
- bounce back from setbacks to keep on track
- live with uncertainty and not be risk averse
- accept that 'stuff happens' and cannot always be prevented.

As a supporting adult find out how you can:

- take a strategic approach to resilience to prepare and protect children
- offer a resilience-friendly environment
- teach children coping strategies to promote personal resilience.

## THE ROOTS OF RESILIENCE

When bad things happen why do some people give up while others carry on? What makes some people feel powerless while others rise to the challenge? What causes some people to be drawn into unhealthy habits like over-eating or drinking to manage stress while others take a healthy approach to stress management? The difference is a set of attitudes and skills called resilience. Resilience is not something you are born with, it is something you develop through personal experience. Resilience can be learned, so what can you do to help children become more resilient?

There are three key ingredients of resilience:

1. a powerful sense of *personal security*, knowing you have a safe haven where you are loved and recognized as an individual

2. *strong self-belief* which makes you aware of and realistic about your personal strengths and competencies

3. a sense of *meaning and purpose* which drives your efforts towards growth and achievement.

When children are small we do everything in our power to protect them from harm. We hope that by protecting them we will give them time to develop the coping strategies to manage both outside dangers and personal disappointments. How can we best do this? What do children need to become able to cope with setbacks?

Resilience can be defined as:

*the ability to thrive, mature and continue to move forward with confidence whatever the prevailing circumstances.*

Resilience is the ability to maintain your personal identity, sense of purpose and belief in your own competence when circumstances are not on your side. This faith in yourself and mental toughness is a multi-layered trait.

## Promoting resilience

What will give a child that personal armoury which will see them through any turbulent times ahead?

A young child naturally has a healthy attitude of curiosity and adventure. Their desire to explore and discover is an essential part of self-discovery and personal development. Children want independence and will try new things. They will resist advice and adult 'interference' and so called early 'behaviour problems' are often related to this tussle for autonomy to give the child the opportunity to try new things.

All adults, whatever their role in a child's life, as a family member or professional, can help children get the balance right between risk and stagnation. For children to flourish, they have to find their strengths and test their potential. They need to make informed decisions about risk and to understand themselves sufficiently to move beyond their comfort zones. This will never be a straightforward, smooth progression, so they also need to know how to deal with setbacks. For the majority of children, the setbacks are likely to be small scale, a matter of dealing with frustration and disappointment in everyday life, rather than needing to draw on deep reserves during a major crisis. What does more commonly affect children is persistent, low-level stress rather than major trauma. Persistent stress can wear you down and affect emotional wellbeing and physical stamina. Children need to learn how to recognize when their pace of life is too frantic. Resilience allows you to recognize when you need to slow down, or say no. Resilience also gives you the determination to keep going with something important when you are tempted to give up.

Protecting children totally from any adversity is practically impossible and psychologically harmful. While you can't predict what life will do, you can offer a child experience to prepare them to be confident and resilient. You cannot easily change the world but you can prepare a child for the world they will live in.

The best preparation for an independent life is one which accepts that there will be ups and downs and where adults offer experience and preparation on a gradual basis. We need to be realistic about what a child can be protected from, and be ready to offer step by step support to build coping strategies until a young person has the maturity and poise to be fully independent.

## Adapting to a changing world

We are living in a century characterized by crises and uncertainty. Both the environment we live in and the economic world we have created for ourselves now seem less under our control. We can no longer turn our back on uncertainty or believe we have sufficient control over events to ensure continued economic growth to ensure an increasing standard of living. The next generation will need to learn to live with uncertainty and have the resilience and creativity to manage any setbacks with practical realism rather than incapacitating anxiety or despair.

## Coping with uncertainty

Despite all the changes going on around us, most people find it difficult to live with uncertainty. We have become more risk averse than previous generations that had no choice. In recent years we have developed the knowledge and the technology to predict more about the world around us. As our expectations of being able to protect ourselves from danger have increased, we have paradoxically become more anxious and less resilient than our ancestors. A report from the Mental Health Foundation in 1999 identified an increased focus on research into risk prevention rather than identifying strategies to promote natural resistance, growth and adaptation.[46]

## A risk-averse society

There is strong evidence that individuals, as well as organizations, are becoming more risk averse and more focused on shielding children from risk. Fewer children are playing outside their homes or in local parks and in many areas local councils are removing play equipment from parks. Some schools are also proscribing activities which may lead to legal action against them in the event of an accident. While this may work for adults in the short term, it fails to teach children to cope with risk and reduces their positive experience of freedom, companionship with peers and creative exciting play.

## Managing fear and uncertainty

Both anxiety and depression are increasing, not only in adults, but also in children and adolescents. The causes of this are complex but undoubtedly people seem to have fewer coping strategies to promote resilience under adverse circumstances. A sense of powerlessness and loss of control underlies depression. If you believe you can't do anything about circumstances which make you unhappy this tends to progress from dissatisfaction into depression. The treatment of depression focuses on helping people to change the habits of thought that embed powerlessness.

Previous generations rarely called upon therapeutic support under adverse circumstances but they did have 'homespun' resilient attitudes and behaviours which are captured in phrases like 'counting your blessings' and 'looking on the bright side'. They anticipated the concept of post-traumatic growth in the phrase 'What doesn't kill you makes you stronger.' In the twenty-first century people are often uncomfortable with these homilies, which can seem rather harsh and unfeeling, but as yet practical knowledge about coping skills to guide people faced with adversity is not widespread.

Many people now see the 'stiff upper lip' approach as restrictive, passive and fatalistic. We are unlikely to turn back the clock and resume the pattern of beliefs and codes of behaviour which our grandparents favoured. What we need now is a revised and updated view of resilience which is more dynamic and in keeping with twenty-first-century attitudes about independence, progress and achievement. Resilience needs to be a strategy which helps us to maintain a flourishing existence whatever the challenges we are facing.

# THE ENVIRONMENTAL BUILDING BLOCKS WHICH SUPPORT RESILIENCE

When children are young, they need adults to manage the environment. Forward planning will allow you to organize things to help children maintain a psychologically healthy, positive balance. Actively preventing children from getting out of their depth in situations they cannot handle will prevent anxiety and frustration, while encouraging them to try activities where small mistakes can be dealt with will build their sense of competence. When children have a positive frame of mind they are not only happier but more able to engage with the world around them so that they learn and grow. The following eight factors support a child's developing resilience.

## 1. Offering security and a safe haven

A child needs to feel secure to adapt to whatever happens around them. Knowing you have people on your side to help when things get tough and to care about you is essential. When a child is feeling fragile because something is difficult or they are feeling unsure how to manage a situation then insecurity will surface. An environment which has built in support will be able to help a child adjust comfortably to challenge. Is there somewhere quiet a child can go to if they are feeling very uncomfortable? How will you offer support to help and reassure a child who feels under threat?

## 2. Providing personal recognition

Feeling safe is vital but feeling recognized and valued goes one step further. As each child discovers and develops their strengths, their sense of who they are and what they are capable of establishes their unique identity. A strong sense of who you are is central to being self-motivated. But a child also needs others to recognize and value them as a unique individual. Recognition is a vital part of belonging. The child knows they have personal qualities which are valued. This supports a child at a deep and satisfying level.

## 3. Accepting difficult feelings

For children to manage their feelings they first need to be heard, understood and to have those feelings validated. Children are naturally more emotionally volatile because their skills of recognizing and managing their feelings are a work in progress. Behaviour coaching provides a systematic way to help a child learn to recognize and manage their feelings.

## 4. Avoiding stress overload

Stress is an imbalance between the demands of the environment and the person's coping capacity. This varies from person to person. Children are more prone to stress overload than adults because of two key factors: lack of control over circumstances and as yet immature development of vital skills and experience. Advance planning can prevent stress overload and also allow a child develop their skills in a graduated way.

## 5. Creating competence and mastery

One of the basic human needs is to feel competent and able to manage the situation you find yourself in. Because children have so much to learn, it is essential to organize situations so that demands are not beyond their reach. Children need to feel competent and capable of mastering situations while also learning new skills. There is a fine balance between moving forward and feeling out of your depth. The answer lies in how adults skilfully manage the environment so that children see that they are making progress.

Children will enjoy using their skills and be keen to progress when goals are realistic. There is a difference between a task which is a stretch and one which produces strain. A successful outcome needs to be possible. Offering an activity which is too far outside a child's comfort zone creates undue pressure which cannot be resolved by effort or persistence. The effect will be frustration and a possible loss of confidence.

## 6. Providing graduated support

A small steps approach encourages gradual progression and builds in success at each stage. All teaching is essentially carefully planned and sequenced activities which guide a child to understand and master new skills. For those outside the teaching profession here is a brief description of what helps divide a task into *small manageable steps*. The process is called task analysis. Take the task you want a child to learn and write down all the steps that are needed to complete it. Then decide whether each step needs to be broken down still further. You can teach the steps in their natural sequence, supporting the later steps so the child remains successful with your help. Making a drink of juice, for example, has the tricky part, pouring accurately, happening at the end. Helping the child pour ensures success. Alternatively you can help with the early stages, reducing help later as needed. Putting on socks is a good example where the later steps are easiest and gathering the sock over your toe at the beginning is more difficult than pulling it up.

## 7. Offering mediation and modelling

Children benefit from seeing how people with experience tackle a task. Observation is useful but rarely sufficient for effective learning. What helps is for adults to talk about and demonstrate how they have done something. Particularly helpful to children is insight into self-management. How do you keep yourself motivated? What do you do to make yourself feel better and to move away from negative moods? Can you offer examples of how you recognize and deal with obstacles?

## 8. Identifying positive role models

Children need the opportunity to look in on other lives and consider what it would be like to be that person. One of the ways for children to have safe, second-hand experience of dealing with tough times is through the positive role models provided by real heroes and fictitious characters. There are currently plenty of opportunities for young people to examine the celebrity lifestyle but much less is said about people who face adversity with strength and determination. Biographies are a rich source of insight for adolescents while younger children can see parallels with their own lives from stories about children (and sometimes animals) facing difficulties and finding ways to overcome them.

## DEVELOPING INDEPENDENT RESILIENCE

If children are to be happy, confident and successful they need the skills to recognize what could sabotage their wellbeing and have the skills to problem solve a situation, to avoid difficulties where possible and to minimize the impact where this is unavoidable.

Resilience may once have been associated with accepting suffering with stoicism, now we should reframe it as the dynamic process of adaptation which provides personal navigation on life's journey. Resilience is essential to a life with ambition, meaning and purpose. Making progress rarely comes without sustained effort, knowing how to successfully avoid any temptations which could take you off course and how to manage the occasional setback. If you are to keep focused on that goal you will need to be able to keep your motivation strong, your energy levels high and recognize any temptations and diversions for what they are. Even with supreme personal self-control and determination there will also be challenges.

## *The ten top skills to build resilience*

Figure 8: The ten top skills to build resilience

### 1. OPTIMIZING PERSONAL STRENGTHS

We saw earlier that Anders Ericsson's research into musical accomplishment identified that the highest performing violin students had put in more hours of practice, around 10,000 hours on average. Theirs was not an achievement that comes from being externally motivated by rewards. The difference in practice time between the groups is likely to be a result of the inner determination that comes from discovering your personal strengths and the joy and passion which accompanies being engaged with something of deep personal significance.

By using their strengths children build their creativity, improve their focused attention skills and experience flow. Another valuable outcome of knowing your personal strengths is the powerful impact on personal identity. 'You are what you do.'

At school children are faced with a set curriculum which decides the skills they are expected to learn at each age and stage of their school career. While schools recognize the diversity among children, the purpose of education is to instil specific knowledge and skills. Children consequently come to measure and compare themselves against these norms. There is a danger that they will undervalue themselves. If education is to fulfil the purpose of 'lighting the fire', each child needs to have a fully rounded picture of themselves and their capabilities.

## 2. POWERFUL PERSONAL GOALS

Children who have their sights set on a goal gain from their motivation and enthusiasm. Jo, aged six, was struggling with writing. He was making good progress with reading, which he found enjoyable, and he wanted to be able to write too but progress was painfully slow. He was happy to sit on his own with a book but looked anxious when asked to write. Jo's mum Rachel wanted to help him at home and wanted to keep it fun. His Aunt Amy and cousin Harry had moved house and were able to visit only occasionally. They kept in touch via video phone and email. Both mums decided to encourage the boys to write and draw pictures and these were then scanned and sent on. Jo was excited to see his work on screen, it boosted his confidence and over the next six months he complained less about writing at school. The sense of purpose he gained by writing letters to his cousin gave him the confidence and resilience to persevere and gradually he found himself making progress.

### Supporting underperforming students

Rory, who was 14 years old, was identified by his school as underperforming. He didn't think he was good at anything and couldn't wait to be allowed to leave. His attendance was poor but sufficient to avoid referral to the school attendance team. In class he was inattentive and created low-level disruption mainly through clowning around. His Head of Year considered he was at risk of poor exam grades at 16 which would then make it likely that he would not go on to further education or training.

Rory told his parents that school was boring and pointless. They realized that he was not fired up by anything, but were unsure what to do. Neither parent had enjoyed school themselves. Rory liked playing football but otherwise had no particular interests. They knew he didn't find lessons enjoyable and that he couldn't see what relevance these subjects had to his daily life. Rory's mum worked in the local supermarket and his dad was a car mechanic. School was seen as an experience to endure rather than one offering significant opportunities.

Rory's form tutor realized that Rory had a little confidence in his capabilities. She arranged for one of the mentors in the learning support team to work with him. He helped Rory identify his personal strengths and to discuss practical ways to use his strengths to increase his sense of competence. Rory's main strength was identified as an interest in how things work; he particularly enjoyed times when he was able to work with his dad on cars or bikes which needed attention. As a younger child he had made quite complex Lego models at school but he thought this was play and had never worked out how to apply these interests to his schoolwork.

School science was mainly theoretical rather than practical and seen by Rory as the preserve of really bright pupils (he called them nerds) who would go to university. Science is essentially about how things work and Rory needed to have that knowledge grounded in relevant and practical experience. Design and technology didn't appeal to him either because of the focus on analytical planning and detailed write ups. At a meeting between school staff and his parents it was agreed to start from where Rory was already gaining enjoyment. Rory would develop some definite projects with his dad. His dad also arranged to take him into work one Saturday morning so he could see the garage during the working day.

At school his mentor would be available for an hour a week to help him research useful material online or approach subject staff for advice. Rory and his dad decided to start by making a radio controlled car which then gave them hours of fun together. Rory's attendance improved and his relationship with staff, helped by his mentor, was more positive. This led to improved classroom behaviour. Both the science and design and technology teams looked at how they could make their subject more accessible and appealing to students who were less academic. Slowly Rory saw these subjects as offering him something too.

When someone is free to decide on their own path in life it is important for them to understand themselves sufficiently well to make good choices. Rory was dissatisfied because he had no faith in his own abilities, but no clear path set for him by family or school. For many disadvantaged young people, particularly those who are no longer with their families and living with foster carers, the risk of feeling purposeless and adrift is particularly high. Having a strong sense of yourself allows you to make informed decisions and have a sense of direction.

## 3. HUMOUR

Resilience depends upon being able to self-manage your feelings and avoid low moods and energy dips. Laughter is a brilliant mood elevator; it is fun at the time and also releases endorphins which sustain positive wellbeing for some time afterwards. Humour can dampen down a sense of gloom and provide a space and time for breaking a low mood. Alongside the physical effect, humour allows us to reframe events in a way which distances us from a situation and can help us to see things differently. Having favourite cartoons or films on DVD can give a child the opportunity to choose to chill out with something that distracts them from thinking about what is bothering them.

Laughter and humour come from within, and are resources to call upon independently. Humour is highly personal and delicate so being told to 'lighten up' or laugh at yourself will often have the opposite effect and make someone feel their concerns are unimportant or inconvenient to others. However, helping children to develop their sense of humour can stand them in good stead when times are tough.

## 4. EXERCISE AND ENERGY BUILDING

Exercise is an important part of the resilience toolkit. It works at several levels so it is important that children get regular daily exercise. The main benefits of exercise are described below:

- Maintaining physical fitness provides the *stamina* needed to sustain effort and is an important part of the resilience toolkit to aid achieving long-term goals. Being too tired to keep going can mean losing momentum at a time when further effort just might move things forward.

- Exercise is also a *mood elevator* so brings benefits on a day to day basis. Children naturally want to be physically active and on the move. Their bodies tell them what they need but unfortunately they are not always able to get active. The demands of schooling and the reduced opportunities for outdoor play from home is affecting children's fitness. Children are recommended to have at least 60 minutes a day of moderate exercise. Exercise is also recommended for adults with mild to moderate depression. The results are as effective as medication, which demonstrates how important it is for wellbeing. Exercise helps to maintain emotional wellbeing and being inactive can soon affect mood and motivation.

- Exercise also *moderates stress* by channelling the stress hormones into activity. Under stress, the sympathetic nervous system prepares the body for activity to address the threat. If this is not burned off through exercise the child will remain tense and liable to aggressive outbursts.

- Exercise creates *energy* which keeps children alert and engaged. Being in the classroom may involve sitting still but concentration and attention are high-energy processes as the brain needs energy to do its work.

Being active on a daily basis allows children to become fit and healthy so that they feel good and can also call upon their energy reserves for whatever they need to do. Children need at least an hour a day of moderate exercise which leaves them slightly breathless. This won't come from walking at an everyday pace but will be provided by active outdoor play and organized sports activities.

## 5. OPTIMISM

What you feel is affected by your thinking. We came across Professor Martin Seligman's work on explanatory style in the previous chapter on learning strengths. Explanatory style is how you make sense of what is happening to you.

There are three dimensions to explanatory style:

- *Optimism* (it will workout well in the end) versus *pessimism* (this can only get worse). Optimism and pessimism are the opposite ends of the attitude spectrum of your feelings about the future.

- *Internal versus external* explanations identifies whether you see an event as under your own control or managed by external forces – what psychologists call your 'locus of control'. Believing that something is not under your control tends to lead to inaction: 'There is nothing I can do about this.' This can result in passivity: 'I'll just wait and see what happens,' or avoidance. 'I'm not going to even try this because I know it won't work,' or even denial. 'This is not happening to me.'

- Whether you consider the situation is *personal, permanent* and *pervasive,* which identifies whether you see the situation as something for which you are directly responsible. If you believe something to be personal you assume you have created or are in some way part of the problem.

For example, Russell was a keen swimmer but had not been performing well in speed trials. He realized that he had got into bad habits, such as staying up late to watch TV in his room, and had also neglected his diet, eating more junk food than was helpful to keep his energy levels high. Russell saw his poor performance as personal but not permanent. He knew he could easily do something about it.

If something is both permanent and pervasive, that is, affecting all aspects of life, you could be in deep trouble. Alice had moved schools recently after having been bullied in her previous school. Her new classmates were curious about her and asked her lots of questions about why she had joined their school. They were not intentionally unfriendly but Alice was on the defensive, she was afraid that they would not like her and that the bullying would start again. Her mother had a more optimistic view; she thought a change of school would solve the problem. She was convinced that the previous school had not managed the situation well and there was a minority bullying culture among a group of disaffected pupils there.

Alice, however, believed it was her fault; she was shy and thought other people found her boring. Alice believed that being popular was very difficult and that you had to be funny, clever, exceptionally pretty and very confident. This perfectionist attitude was unhelpful. Alice thought she was none of those things and that things would go wrong when other people realized. Because she was fearful of what people thought, she was evasive when people talked to her, and rarely smiled or took a reciprocal interest in others. People did begin to think that Alice was unfriendly and not interested in them, as she rarely gave anything back to the conversation. It was becoming a self-fulfilling prophecy.

Alice's Head of Year was aware of Alice's unease and the reasons for her move. She had given Alice some time to settle in naturally, but saw this was not working and quickly convened a meeting between Alice's parents, herself and the form tutor. They agreed some strategies to help Alice relax and be friendlier. She was invited to join a lunchtime club which offered an informal setting for supporting less socially confident pupils. As well as free time to chat to each other, there were some informal ice breakers and games to build friendship skills. Alice benefited from looking at what she could do to find new friends. Her attitude became more optimistic and she no longer believed that the situation was personal and permanent. Alice now has a group of friends and is enjoying her new school.

## 6. CHALLENGING UNHELPFUL THINKING

Professor Martin Seligman and his colleagues at Pennsylvania State University in the United States have developed a programme for schools which offers group training to young people to help them challenge pessimistic thoughts and develop a more optimistic approach to life. There is a strong link between a pessimistic explanatory style and the development of depression.

Depression is a state of low mood which persists over several weeks without lifting; it differs from periodic dips in wellbeing and is accompanied by low energy and inertia. Someone who is depressed believes that circumstances are beyond their control. A full account of the Penn Resilience Project and the ABCDE approach to developing resilience can be found in *The Optimistic Child* by Martin Seligman.[47] The ABCDE approach is a logical and structured approach which can be taught to individual children.

This five-part system teaches a child how to identify patterns of thought which are pessimistic and unhelpful. A child can learn how to replace unhelpful beliefs with more optimistic and energizing statements which encourage them to take action. Depressed thinking is characterized by stagnation and passivity which further embeds the sense of hopelessness. Children learn to identify ways of increasing their understanding of unhelpful thinking and to use problem solving techniques to change their thinking and their behaviour:

### A is for antecedents

The first part of the process is to look carefully at what has happened. Let's meet Daniel who is worrying about his popularity with his peers. Daniel wasn't invited to join Mark, his best friend, on a trip to the park with a group of friends. Daniel felt upset and betrayed. He wondered whether this was a sign that Mark was tired of their friendship.

### B is for belief

Daniel's mother listened sympathetically as he told her about what had happened. She acknowledged his feelings were hurt and asked him if he could tell her some of the thoughts which were going through his head. She explained that sometimes if we stop what we are doing and are quiet we can become more aware of the thoughts and ideas which pop in to our heads. Daniel said he thought that best friends should always want to be together.

## C is for Consequences

Daniel's belief led him to feel rejected and to see this as both personal but possibly permanent too. If Mark didn't want to be his friend perhaps other people would feel the same and he would never have a best friend again (pervasive thinking).

## D is for Disputation

Daniel's mother helped him to dispute these pessimistic thoughts. Did Daniel only want to spend time with Mark? No he sometimes enjoyed being in a group too. Daniel played in a Sunday football team where he had a different set of friends. He enjoyed their company without Mark. She helped Daniel to think about what was special about the friendship with Mark and what they had in common. She also encouraged him to see that their closeness was different to mixing in a group and it was hard to do both together.

## E is for Energizing

Daniel decided that he and Mark enjoyed being together, just the two of them. They could also enjoy other friends in a group. When he next saw Mark he was able to ask how the trip to the park went without sounding jealous or annoyed.

## When can you use the ABCDE approach?

The ABCDE approach works well for children from eight years old onwards. Being aware of what has triggered a low mood is difficult for children under that age who have not as yet developed sufficient meta-cognitive skills to think about their thinking.

Adults supporting younger children could offer observations: 'I see you are feeling very angry,' 'I know you don't like it when your sister borrows your toys,' 'I wonder if that has made you upset?'

## 7. POSITIVITY

Resilience would be rather grim and joyless if it depended on a rigid determination to keep the show on the road under adversity. Resilience is also about perspective and balance. How serious is what is happening, is it a catastrophe or merely a frustration? Positivity, which we explored in an earlier chapter, is a resilient mindset which you can actively cultivate to retain the healthy 3:1 ratio of positive to negative emotions. Three key approaches which build positivity are gratitude, appreciation and savouring. Gratitude and appreciation support resilience by focusing our attention on what is working well for us.

## 8. AVOIDING TEMPTATION

Resilience includes the ability to say no. Self-control is a valuable skill which allows you to resist temptation. The five-year-olds who were able to wait 15 minutes to have their two marshmallows, rather than take one immediately, had fewer behaviour problems and were doing better at school when revisited some years later. Small children are generally very easily sidetracked so this was a tough task for them. Children who learn to master their impulses can more easily maintain their focus on a task which is difficult or challenging.

## 9. PERSISTENCE

Persistence can be the difference between giving in and carrying on. It can differentiate those with talent who keep on perfecting their skill and those who lose heart. Thomas Edison, who invented the light bulb after many prototypes had failed, is supposed to have said 'I have not failed. I have just found 10,000 ways that won't work.'

The impact of persistence on performance has recently been confirmed in research with undergraduates to identify what measures best predict high performance. Traditionally measures like cognitive ability and exam results in school have been the focus of assessment. However, Angela Duckworth, a student of Martin Seligman's, hypothesized that character traits such as persistence would also be relevant. Her research is described in *Flourish*, Seligman's most recent book. Duckworth found that high-performing undergraduates can be predicted from scores on a test of 'grit' and persistence. At every level of ability the 'grittier' students obtained the highest grades. This finding has also been replicated with those undertaking military training and serves as a good predictor of those who will stay the course in the US special forces training, the equivalent of the UK SAS.

## 10. PROBLEM SOLVING

Having a strategy to manage situations which cannot be resisted or avoided is essential. This helps to minimize the impact and to create control over the course of the adversity. Effective problem solving requires emotional acceptance of the realities of the situation as well as a rational analysis of what is happening and how best to move forward.

## BOX 13   THE SEVEN-STEP RESILIENCE RECOVERY PROGRAMME

The Seven-step Resilience Recovery Programme is clear and simple to remember.

### 1. What is happening?

A clear and realistic overview will help someone to stand back from the situation and look at the whole picture. When you are enmeshed in a problem it can be hard to distance yourself and think clearly. Using techniques like visualizing yourself on a balcony looking down on your current situation, identifying exactly what is happening can help you to dissociate. Writing a letter to an imaginary friend to explain what is going on can also be helpful.

### 2. What do I want to be different?

You may have an inner voice saying 'It shouldn't be happening to me' but people who are resilient will also be saying 'What can I do about it?' They accept that upsetting as it is, they have to take action.

### 3. What parts are beyond my control?

In a crisis people tend to look for someone to blame or someone to come and rescue them. They look for an external solution. A lot of time and energy can be used up in seeking an external solution. Focusing on solutions which are not within your control can embed the sense of helplessness. Acknowledging the constraints is essential before you can start your plan. What can I change?

### 4. How do I feel right now?

Whether you are angry, sad or fearful you need to be aware of those feelings and the extent to which they can make it hard to think straight. Powerful feelings can be physically draining, too, leaving you tired or easily distracted. Accepting the ups and downs will help you set realistic goals for yourself.

### 5. Who can help me?

Having someone to talk to and give you encouragement supports you at several levels. It provides emotional support, gives you a sounding board for your ideas and can provide useful feedback. You can also set small-step goals which you know you can manage and have someone on your team to cheer you on when these seem too difficult. This is very different from looking for someone to do it for you.

### 6. What is my first step?

The first step is the most important, but in many ways it doesn't matter what it is. Just do it, as the saying goes. The important thing is to get started, and not to ruminate or procrastinate searching out the perfect solution.

### 7. Review progress

Go back through the six preceding steps to evaluate where things are and plan the next move. Repeat this process as many times as necessary.

## USING THE SEVEN-STEP PROGRAMME

### Resilience and recovery

Jack had a serious skateboarding accident which left him with concussion and some memory loss. He missed several weeks at school before returning to lessons. However, once back at school he found his attention was poor, and he became easily distracted. He was finding it difficult to tune into lessons and follow the teacher. He was told that he had some bruising to the brain which would take some time to settle down. Jack felt very low and worried about what life was going to be like. He became rather distant with his friends, and bad tempered at home. His family began to worry that his head injury had caused a personality change. Jack was referred to an educational psychologist by the school with a view to assessing his memory difficulties. She decided that, as medical reports suggested, this was a temporary situation and it might be of more value to help Jack strengthen his coping strategies. She used the seven-step plan to help Jack explore how to manage his changed circumstances.

Together they discussed the facts of the situation; medical reports showed that there were some changes which were unpleasant but likely to be temporary. Jack admitted he was worrying that this might not be true. He had heard his parents talking to the consultant about the worst case scenario and had wondered what that meant.

Jack decided he wanted to be able to manage his learning better. He would need to be more open with people about his difficulties in lessons. He was afraid they would think he had permanent brain damage and he couldn't cope with talking about this. Jack thought that his anger was probably related to this, and that he would feel happier if he was more able to cope on a daily basis.

Getting better was going to take time but Jack was encouraged to set himself small goals to monitor improvements. The learning support coordinator in the school was clearly the right person to ask for support. Jack agreed that the psychologist could share their discussions with her and ask her to meet with Jack to set up some support in class.

Jack agreed to have one of her team shadow him for half a day. The support assistant noticed he was distracted and did not cope well in a few lessons which needed high levels of listening. He did not take notes, as previously he had found no problem following what was said. It was arranged for Jack to be given a lesson outline for those subjects and he would take key word notes or use a mind mapping approach. Once Jack had some useful strategies he felt much calmer and more hopeful. Over the course of the term his stamina improved but he continued to use the learning strategies as they had proved useful.

## Behaviour change

Jason, aged 15, was not able to live with his family but remained hopeful that with the help of his social worker he would be able to return home. His mother was a single parent with two younger children. Jason had come into care on a voluntary basis when his antisocial behaviour and binge drinking had created problems. His group of friends drank heavily and got into trouble for vandalism and had also targeted a vulnerable family. Windows had been broken and the family were taunted and intimidated when they came outside. Jason's mother had pressure from her neighbours to discipline him but she found him threatening to her and his younger siblings. His father had left when he was small and had no contact with the family. His mother thought Jason was taking after his father and felt helpless about what to do if he had inherited his character from his father.

When he first came into care Jason was extremely angry with his mother and his neighbours. He was unable to see himself as responsible in any way and expected all the changes to come from others. He saw his social worker's role as sorting it all out for him so he could go home and pick up where he left off. His inability to see a situation from other perspectives left the situation stuck. For change to happen Jason needed to understand things differently.

His social worker focused on two questions, one involving 'away from' motivation and the other involving positive attraction:

- What was missing in his current life that he wanted to add which would make his life better?

- What did he want to get away from in his current life?

Jason accepted that getting out of care was important to him as was being on better terms with his family. If he wanted those things he had to find a way to make that happen. They were then able to use the seven-step problem solving technique to make a start. It was not a quick process and he needed support to explore other people's perspectives on what was happening. Jason's relationship with the family was precarious and family therapy helped to address this, including helping his mother to see how she could help him. He had regular contact with his younger siblings and began to enjoy their company rather than see them as nuisances.

## SUMMARY

- Resilience is a set of attitudes and skills which enable you to navigate your way through life with optimism and the fortitude to manage adversity.

- The three key ingredients of resilience: personal security, strong self-belief and a sense of meaning and purpose provide the foundations on which to build effective coping strategies and problem solving skills.

- Children need an environment which protects them while they mature and which also helps them to develop the skills and the knowledge to make good choices and cope with adversity.

- Ten skills can be used to help people to manage adversity and make constructive changes. These include optimizing personal strengths, working towards meaningful goals and developing optimism and positivity.

- The Seven-step Resilience Recovery Programme is designed for young people who are having difficulties and need help to develop the skills they need to recover their poise and face the future well prepared for any future challenges.

# Developing Independence
## The Journey through Childhood

Psychological wellbeing is a set of skills which help a young person to navigate their way in life. They will understand themselves better, know what suits them and what they want from life. They will have the skills to make good choices, avoid temptations and create a life that brings happiness and fulfilment.

The path to maturity and independence is not a short one and twists and turns are inevitable along the way. Independence is gained little by little from both practice and experience.

## THE FLOURISHING PROGRAMME

Before you begin to use the Flourishing Programme with a child here is an overview of some of the evidence from Positive Psychology which lies behind the Flourishing Programme.

### 1. Optimism

Optimism is a faith in the future which comes from confidence in yourself and others. It is not a passive, blind faith that assumes destiny is predetermined, it is more of an active and energetic viewpoint based on self-knowledge and positive past experience. It is not a perspective on life that is established easily. The negativity bias which results from our protective emotions sensing a potential threat will tend to pop up now and then. However, optimism is essential to challenge this innate pessimism and sustain growth.

### 2. Focus on strengths

Strengths have both a skill component – you are confident of your performance – and an emotional component – you find working with your strengths enjoyable and satisfying. Strengths therefore provide a deep and lasting sense of fulfilment.

### 3. Motivation

Finding a powerful sense of meaning and purpose in what you do makes the difference between drifting along and going somewhere. Self Determination Theory suggests we have a natural drive towards competence and a need for autonomy which impels us to work towards goals which reflect who we are.

### 4. Self-belief

Confidence in yourself comes from how you explain what happens to you – your explanatory style. Positive self-belief is nourished by an optimistic perspective which assumes you have the control to make constructive changes. A perceived lack of control underlies mental health difficulties such as anxiety disorders and depression.

### 5. Set goals

Finding a purpose, whether in one area of your life like a hobby, or routinely in relation to school work makes young people happier and more confident. Goals should be positively phrased and based on personal progress targets – so you can aim for self-improvement rather than competition with peers. Evidence suggests that writing goals down increases the likelihood of both compliance and better outcomes. Personal goal setting also builds a young person's awareness of what they want and what they are capable of. Setting goals also provides feedback on what is realistic as young people adjust their expectations in line with progress.

### 6. Adopt a growth mindset

Learning is a skill rather than a fixed ability. This perspective on learning encourages optimism, effort and persistence which are essential for optimal progress.

### 7. Positivity

This is an active process of creating opportunities for personal enjoyment and fulfilling relationships. It is also a way of looking at the world with a positive perspective which encourages the search for opportunities. Because the emotions of love and enjoyment are outnumbered by the protective emotions which create anger, fear and anxiety a positivity ratio of 3:1 not only makes people feel better but helps them make good choices which avoid temptations.

## 8. Circles of support

Psychological wellbeing is not about rugged individualism – one person fulfilling their own desires. Happy people have a strong network of both close relationships and supportive friendships. Young people need to balance their need for independence with the valuable support of close relationships.

## 9. Appreciation

Young people can find themselves preoccupied with a raft of expectations and goals for the future. While knowing where you are going is essential for progress, taking time to appreciate what is good in your life now is very grounding. Mindfulness – an ability to focus intently in the moment – has been found to offer huge benefits in reducing anxiety and creating a calmer, more relaxed experience.

## 10. Gratitude

Linked to appreciation, gratitude is an awareness of what you have in your life which is good and which nurtures your wellbeing. Gratitude towards others can be challenging for young people because dependence on the other person can make them feel unsure of how capable and in control they are. As young people become more confident of their own abilities they become less ambivalent towards expressing gratitude to others. Perhaps when young people can easily and spontaneously express gratitude we will know that they are well on their way to independent psychological wellbeing

> **BOX 14  TEN STRATEGIES TO HELP YOU MAKE THE FLOURISHING PROGRAMME A SUCCESS**
>
> **1. Look at the world through the child's eyes**
>
> It is important to be aware of both how a child is feeling and what practical skills and thinking strategies are needed to manage a situation successfully. What will work best for them?

### 2. Set realistic expectations

Expectations should be based on both what suits the child and what their age and stage of development will allow. Child-development norms are now widely available from books and online. However one note of caution about age-related norms. The figure quoted will be an average but the variation will be wide: children can be ahead in some areas and less so in others. Aim not to set expectations which are too big a stretch for a child.

### 3. Warmth and rapport

These are the top qualities which you can use to influence others and sustain relationships. Children look for positive and constructive feedback to let them know how they are progressing. Aim for a positivity ratio of 3:1 to create that feel good factor.

### 4. Enlist support

There is a saying that it a takes a village to raise a child. I think that is true not only for the child but for the adults who are responsible for the child's welfare. You need others to turn to who can step in at a practical level or just listen and let you let off steam. For more specific support with using the Flourishing Programme consider linking up with a buddy for mutual support. See co-coaching section below.

### 5. Discover and use your own personal strengths

Working to your own strengths provides a great role model for children but also encourages you to discover what works for you and gives you satisfaction. Doing what you know you do well boosts confidence and also brings out your creative side to find solutions to situations which are challenging.

### 6. Create strong boundaries

These keep a child within their zone of competence. Firm boundaries are like scaffolding, providing support until a child demonstrates sufficient knowledge, skills and maturity to handle the situation independently. Strong boundaries reduce the risk of failure and frustration and raise the chances of success.

### 7. Provide lots of supported practice

Most children now grow up in small families and spend their days in school with others the same age. The opportunities for learning by observation and example can be narrower now than in previous generations when children played outside in mixed age groups. Children need adults to help them meet situations where their skills can be practised safely and where they can find success.

### 8. Accept mistakes

Progress rarely goes in a straight line. When things don't go according to plan we can either become frustrated and demotivated or we can explore what this tells us to help us decide what to do next. A growth mindset helps a child live with mistakes and profit from them.

### 9. Be aware of other influences

Role models shape children's thinking and aspirations. They are not always positive. They can either inspire and inform or make children feel dissatisfied with themselves. The peer group is hugely important as a source of belonging and for building identity but can also play upon a child's vulnerabilities. Similarly the media offers images which attract a young person but if they are too far out of reach they cause deep dissatisfaction. You can help them consider and make sense of these influences for themselves. Equally, you can draw attention to role models who are resilient, or very optimistic or passionate about doing something well.

### 10. Celebrate success

When you focus on what is happening right now rather than any lengthy 'to do list' you start to notice what is going well and what you can savour and feel grateful for. Young people need to develop the habit of being in the moment and appreciating what is happening around them and what they are capable of contributing.

## WORKING WITH A BUDDY: HOW CO-COACHING CAN INCREASE YOUR SUCCESS WITH THE FLOURISHING PROGRAMME

There is strong evidence that people make more progress and stay motivated for longer when they have social support. If you are using the Flourishing Programme for the first time why not find someone who is also starting out. The children you work with may be very different but there are huge advantages to taking time to compare notes and share ideas.

Co-coaching is a relationship where two people share progress reports and help each other to problem solve issues. It is important that you ensure confidentiality and agree to focus on positive feedback. The advantages of co-coaching are that you can:

- celebrate progress and give mutual support at regular agreed intervals
- discuss problem areas and help each other to identify options to address the issues
- keep your motivation high when you need an energy boost
- identify small steps of progress when working with a complex situation
- be more creative when new ideas are needed
- learn from each other and appreciate the skill and commitment each of you brings to supporting a child.

Nurturing a child's wellbeing is the best gift you can give them. It is a gift they can take with them throughout life. You are teaching a child how to be happy and what to do to manage disappointments. You are helping a child to discover and use their strengths so they feel competent and able to make choices to give life purpose and satisfaction. You are empowering them to be optimistic and positive so that life is exciting and full of hope. From you they have learned the value of positive communication and how to make enduring relationships. You have given them the confidence to be themselves and to follow their dreams. You are changing the world one child at a time.

# Notes

1 Seligman, M. (2002) *Authentic Happiness: Using the New Positive Psychology to Realize your Potential for Lasting Fulfilment.* Australia: Random House.

2 World Health Organization (2005) *Promoting Mental Health.* Geneva: World Health Organization.

3 Lyubomirsky, S. (2007) *The How of Happiness.* London: Sphere.

4 UNICEF (2007) *Child Poverty in Perspective. An Overview of Child Wellbeing in Rich Countries.* New York: UNICEF.

5 Layard, R. and Dunn, J. (2009) *A Good Childhood, Searching for Values in a Competitive Age.* London: Penguin Books.

6 Seligman, M. (1990) *Learned Optimism: How to Change your Mind and your Life.* New York: Vintage.

7 Maslow, A. (1954) *Motivation and Personality.* New York: Harper and Row.

8 Seligman, M. (2002) *Authentic Happiness: Using the New Positive Psychology to Realize your Potential for Lasting Fulfilment.* Australia: Random House.

9 Seligman, M. (2011) *Flourish: A Visionary New Understanding of Happiness and Wellbeing and How to Achieve Them.* Boston: Nicholas Brealey Publishing.

10 Pink, D. (2009) *Drive: The Surprising Truth about What Motivates Us.* Edinburgh: Canongate.

11 Quart, A. (2006) *Hothouse Kids: How the Pressure to Succeed Is Threatening Childhood.* New York: Arrow.

12 www.vanessamaeonline.com/articles/mirror.html

13 Honore, C. (2004) *In Praise of Slow.* London: Orion.

14 Covey, S. (1997) *The 7 Habits of Highly Effective Families.* New York: Simon and Schuster.

15 Pink, D. (2009) *Drive: The Surprising Truth about What Motivates Us.* Edinburgh: Canongate.

16 This test is available free online at www.authentichappiness.org, accessed November 2011.

17 Linley, A., Willars, J. and Biswas-Diener, R. (2010) *The Strengths Book.* Coventry: CAPP Press.

18 Gardner, H. (1993) *Frames of Mind.* London: Fontana.

19 *Jo Frost's Extreme Parental Guidance,* Channel 4, August 2011.

20 Fox, J. (2008) *Your Child's Strengths: A Guide for Parents and Teachers.* London: Viking Penguin.

21 Linley, A., Willars, J. and Biswas-Diener, R. (2010) *The Strengths Book.* Coventry: CAPP Press.

22 www.nhs.uk/change4life, accessed November 2011.

23 Fox-Eades, J. (2008) *Celebrating Strengths: Building Strengths Based Schools.* Coventry: CAPP Press.

24 Described in Goleman, D. (1996) *Emotional Intelligence.* London: Bloomsbury, p. 27.

25  Freud, S. (1953–1974) *The Standard Edition of the Complete Psychological Works of Sigmund Freud.* (J. Strachey, ed. and trans.) London: Hogarth Press.

26  The internal working model was first described by John Bowlby in his work on attachment. Sue Gerhardt's (2004) *Why Love Matters: How Affection Shapes a Baby's Brain.* London: Routledge, provides a good overview of current research on a child's emotional development.

27  Jonathan Haidt uses this metaphor in his 2006 book *The Happiness Hypothesis.* New York: Arrow.

28  The marshmallow test reproduced by Dr David Walsh on YouTube demonstrates four-year-old children attempting to wait. www.youtube.com/watch?v=amsqeYOk--w.

29  Reported in Seligman, M. (2011) *Flourish: A Visionary New Understanding of Happiness and Wellbeing and How to Achieve Them.* Boston: Nicholas Brealey Publishing.

30  Grenville-Cleave, B. and Boniwell, I. (2008) *The Happiness Equation.* Avon, MA: Adams Media.

31  Lyubomirsky, S. (2007) *The How of Happiness.* London: Sphere.

32  Fredrickson, B. (2009) *Positivity: Groundbreaking Research to Release your Inner Optimist and Thrive.* Oxford: Oneworld.

33  Goleman, D. (2006) *Social Intelligence: The New Science of Social Relationships.* New York: Arrow.

34  Gerhardt, G. (2004) *Why Love Matters: How Affection Shapes a Baby's Brain.* London: Routledge.

35  For Alan Schore's research into the neuropsychology of brain development, see Gerhardt, *Why Love Matters* (note 34).

36  The three good things exercise is a powerful technique to increase wellbeing. Every night for one week look back at your day and find three things that went well for you. Write them down and reflect on your role. Both the writing down and the reflection have been shown to be essential to impact on wellbeing. See Boniwell, I. (2006) *Positive Psychology in a Nutshell.* London: PWCB.

37  Bronson, P. and Merryman, A. (2009) Chapter 10 'Why Hannah Talks and Alyssa Doesn't.' In *Nurture Shock.* London: Ebury Press.

38  Wood, D. (1988) *How Children Think and Learn.* Oxford: Blackwell.

39  Martin Seligman describes this work in his latest book *Flourish,* see note 29. I have developed the table to illustrate each response style.

40  James, W. (1890) *The Principles of Psychology.* Boston, MA: Henry Holt.

41  Coffield, R. *et al.* (2004) *Learning Styles and Pedagogy, a Systematic and Critical Review.* London: Learning Skills Research Centre.

42  Dweck, C. (2007) *Mindset: The New Psychology of Success.* New York: Ballantine Books.

43  Seligman, M. with Reivich, K., Jaycox, L. and Gillham, J. (2007) *The Optimistic Child: A Proven Program to Safeguard Children against Depression and Build Lifelong Resilience.* New York: Houghton Mifflin Books.

44  Pink, D. (2009) *Drive: The Surprising Truth about What Motivates Us.* Edinburgh: Canongate.

45  As described by Martin Seligman in *Flourish,* p. 115 (see note 29).

46  The Mental Health Foundation (1999) *Bright Futures: Protecting Children and Young People's Mental Health.* London: Mental Health Foundation.

47  Seligman, M. with Reivich, K., Jaycox, L. and Gillham, J. (2007) *The Optimistic Child: A Proven Program to Safeguard Children against Depression and Build Lifelong Resilience.* New York: Houghton Mifflin Books.

# Index